# Saronic Gulf Islands, Greece.

## Travel Guide

Author
Michael Lopez

**Publisher**:
INFORMATION-SOURCE
16192 Coastal Highway
Lewes, DE 19958. U.S.A.

# Table of Content

# Summary

Saronic Gulf Islands: It is regretting that certain people have a mindset that traveling is a waste of time, energy and money. Some also find traveling an extremely boring activity. Nevertheless, a good majority of people across the world prefer traveling, rather than staying inside the confined spaces of their homes. They love to explore new places, meet new people, and see things that they would not find in their homelands. It is this very popular attitude that has made tourism, one of the most profitable, commercial sectors in the world.

People travel for various reasons. Some travel for work, others for fun, and some for finding mental peace. Though every person may have his/her own reason to go on a journey, it is essential to note that traveling, in itself, has some inherent advantages. For one, for some days getting away from everyday routine is a pleasant change. It not only refreshes one's body, but also mind and soul. Traveling to a distant place and doing exciting things that are not thought of otherwise, can rejuvenate a person, who then returns home, ready to take on new and more difficult challenges in life and work. It makes a person forget his worries, problems, frustrations, and fears, albeit for some time. It gives him a chance to think wisely and constructively. Traveling also helps to heal; it can mend a broken heart.

For many people, traveling is a way to attain knowledge, and perhaps, a quest to find answers to their questions. For this, many people prefer to go to faraway and isolated places. For believers, it is a search for God and to gain higher knowledge; for others, it is a search for inner peace. They might or might not find what they are looking for, but such an experience certainly enriches their lives.

Celebrating: There's always a happy reason to take a trip. It could be a landmark birthday or anniversary. A graduation. A wedding or pre-wedding festivities. Even a babymoon before a little one arrives. A special occasion is made even more special by celebrating away from the hectic pace of life at home. It's also a good way to gather family and friends from distant corners to mark the milestone. Celebration vacations provide a lasting benefit as well: shared memories for a lifetime.

Saronic Gulf Islands, Greece

# Saronic Gulf Islands Tourism
## Introduction

Located just off the mainland of Greece, the Saronic Gulf Islands are a group of islands bordered by the Aegean Sea. Easily accessible by boat and hydrofoil, services to the Saronic Gulf Islands operate from Piraeus and the Peloponnese. A popular holiday destination for international visitors and Greeks alike, the islands are known for their beautiful natural paradise, crystal waters, idyllic beaches, pristine hillsides, rugged mountains and a lively cosmopolitan atmosphere. Some of the most popular islands include Aegina, Poros, Idra and Spetses. Use the Saronic Gulf map below to explore regions of the city, or choose your accommodation with the help of our handy hotel map.

They could easily fill a holiday on their own but, combined with Athens and the mainland, would make for a trip that summed up the very best of Greece.

4

Having said that, and unless you're keen to see the site where the Greeks defeated the Persian navy in 480 BC, Salamis is probably not worth the effort. Aegina (an hour by ferry from Athens) is a much better bet. The classical temple of Aphaea is everything you imagine a Greek temple to be and is far less visited than some.

Heading south around the Peloponnese coast, the islands become more upmarket and expensive, and are best out of season. Poros, only a long stone's throw from the mainland, attracts some package tourism but is beautiful, nonetheless, and a great base for exploring the famous sites on the mainland (the theatre of Epidaurus and Mycenae among them).

Hydra ramps up the stakes, not even allowing cars or bicycles to spoil the island's tranquillity. If you can afford it, its charms are obvious and have not gone unnoticed by the world's artists, writers and musicians.

Spetses, a little further on, is an outpost for the remaining rich Greeks and the yacht crowd. Away from them, the interior is almost entirely unpopulated and hiking will allow you to savour the mysterious atmosphere that inspired John Fowles' The Magus. Lastly, Kythira is strictly part of the Ionian islands, but is most easily reached from the Peloponnese. If you can make it here, you will be rewarded with one of the most authentic and beautiful Greek islands there is.

# Saronic Gulf Islands Travel Guide

Aegina is a paradise for nature lovers with many forests, traditional mountain villages and beautiful beaches. This island enjoys a beautiful mild climate and it is famous for its pistachio nuts and pottery. The most important archaeological site lies to the east of the island, where the temple of Aphaia is situated.

Aegina town, a charming bustling port, is the largest settlement. It has many seafront restaurants offering fresh seafood meals at reasonable prices. Here you can enjoy this picturesque port of the island and neo-classical buildings dating back to the newborn Greek State in 1828.

Other places of interest include the monastery of Agios Nectarios - the patron of the island. Agia Marina is the most popular beach of the island full of pine trees reaching the waterfront.

Poros is known for its untouched hillsides, crystal clear waters and idyllic beaches. A small channel separates the island from mainland Peloponesse and can be crossed easily by a small boat or even swimming. Poros town is a pretty and serene place with unbroken views across terracotta-tiled roofs. As you travel through the city, you will get to see a naval station, the clock tower, the ruins of a sanctuary dedicated to Poseidon, a large city library and the archaeological museum.

Neorio village is northwest of Poros town. It is the island's main tourist resort with many hotels, shops and tavernas. The golden sand and numerous pine trees make this beach one of the most beautiful on the island.

Hydra's natural ascending harbour and ragged landscape has inspired artists since the early 1800s. A favourite weekend escape for the Athenians this cosmopolitan island attracts many visitors worldwide. Known for its naval tradition Hydra has many colourful old mansions. These originally belonged to the families of captains who were involved in the Greek Revolution of 1821 against Turkey.

No vehicles are allowed in Idra and the main mode of transport for tourists is donkeys and mules. Boats and water taxis are used to visit the many secluded bays of this delightful island. Ideal for those who enjoy a relaxing lifestyle and for art lovers who can explore the many galleries of the island.

Spetses is also famous for its place in the 1821 Greek Revolution. Like in Idra, private cars are not permitted on this island so travel is by horse drawn carriages or the local bus. A boat tour around the

7

island is available during the tourist season, which includes a swim at one of the many sandy beaches of Spetses.

This island offers the visitor tranquillity combined with a lively cosmopolitan life. Dapia, the island's port, is full of tavernas and bars but as one moves inland the natural beauty of the island comes alive.

## Things to Do in Saronic Islands

The islands of the Saronic Gulf are so close to Athens that each summer Athenians flee there for some relief from the heat and the crowds. The summer of 2007 was the hottest in at least 90 years . . . until the summer of 2010! If these summer scorchers continue, more and more Athenians will try to escape the pulverizing heat of Athens on as many summer weekends as possible. These islands are also popular destinations for European and American travelers with limited time, who are determined not to go home without seeing at least one Greek island.

The easiest island to visit is Aegina, just 30km (17 nautical miles) from Piraeus. The main attractions in addition to the ease of the journey are the Doric Temple of Aphaia, one of the best-preserved Greek temples; several good beaches; and verdant pine and pistachio groves. That's the good news. The bad news is that Aegina is so close to Athens and Piraeus that it's become a bedroom suburb for Athens, with many of its 10,000 inhabitants commuting to work by boat. That said, Aegina town still has its pleasures, and the Temple of Aphaia and deserted medieval town of Paleohora are terrific. If you come here, try to avoid weekends and the month of August.

Poros is hardly an island at all; only a narrow (370m/1,214-ft.) inlet separates it from the Peloponnese. There are several decent beaches, and the landscape is wooded, gentle, and rolling, like the landscape of the adjacent mainland. Alas, Poros's pine groves were badly damaged by the summer fires of 2007, and still recovering. Poros is popular with tour groups as well as young Athenians (in part because the Naval Cadets' Training School here means that there are lots of young men eager to party). On summer nights, the waterfront is either very lively or hideously crowded, depending on your point of view.

Hydra (Idra), with its bare hills, superb natural harbor, and elegant stone mansions, is the most strikingly beautiful of the Saronic Gulf islands. One of the first Greek islands to be "discovered" by artists, writers, and bons vivants in the '50s, Hydra is not the place to experience traditional village life. The island has been declared a national monument, from which cars have been banished, but its relative quiet is increasingly being infiltrated by motorcycles. A major drawback: Few of the beaches are good for swimming, although you can swim from the rocks in and just out of Hydra town.

Spetses has always been popular with wealthy Athenians, who built and continue to build handsome villas. If you like wooded islands, you'll love Spetses, although summer forest fires over the last few years have destroyed some of its pine groves.

You can make a day trip to any of the islands, and some day cruises out of Piraeus rush you on and off three of them, usually with quick stops at Hydra, Poros, and Spetses. If you plan to spend the night in summer, book *well* in advance. The website *(windmillstravel.com)* is a useful resource for all the islands..

If you go to one of these islands on a day trip, remember that, unlike the more sturdy ferries, hydrofoils cannot travel when the sea is rough. You may find yourself an overnight island visitor, grateful to be given the still-warm bed in a private home surrendered by a family member to make some money. (I speak from experience.) *Greek Island Hopping,* published annually by Thomas Cook, is, by its own admission, out of date by the time it sees print. Still, it's a very useful volume for finding out where (if not when) you can travel among the Greek islands.

If possible, avoid June through August, unless you have a hotel reservation and think that you'd enjoy the hustle and bustle of high season. Also, mid-July through August, boats leaving Piraeus for the islands are heavily booked often seriously overbooked. It is sometimes possible to get a deck passage without a reservation, but even that can be difficult when as many as 100,000 Athenians leave Piraeus on a summer weekend. Most ships will not allow passengers to board without a ticket.

And remember: Some hydrofoils leave from the Piraeus Main Harbor while others leave from the Piraeus Marina Zea Harbor and some leave from both harbors! It's a good idea to arrive early, in case your boat is leaving from a different spot from the one you expect.

## Aegina

Aegina, Modern Greek Aíyina, island, one of the largest in the Saronic group of Greece, about 16 miles (26 km) south-southwest of Piraeus. With an area of about 32 square miles (83 square km), it is an eparkhía (eparchy) of the nomós (department) of Piraeus. The northern plains and hills are cultivated with vines and olive, fig, almond, and pistachio trees, while along the east coast stretches a ridge of light volcanic rock known as trachyte. The highest point is conical Mount Áyios Ilías (ancient Mount Pan Hellenion), at 1,745

11

feet (532 metres). On the west coast the chief town and port, Aegina, lies over part of the ancient town of the same name.

Inhabited since Neolithic times (c. 3000 BCE), the island became a leading maritime power after the 7th century BCE because of its strategic position, and its silver coins became currency in most of the Dorian states. Aegina's economic rivalry with Athens led to wars and to its close collaboration with Persia, but at the Battle of Salamis (480 BCE) the island sided with Athens and prevailed. The conspicuous bravery of the tiny Aeginetan contingent (only about 40 ships) was recognized by a prize for valour. Hostility with Athens was later resumed, and at the beginning of the Peloponnesian War the Athenians deported all of Aegina's population and replaced them with Athenian settlers (431 BCE). The Spartans settled the refugees in the region of Thyreatis in northern Laconia.

The remnants were allowed to return from exile in 404 BCE after the defeat of Athens, but Aegina never recovered from the blow. It fell with the rest of Greece to Macedon and then to the Romans in 133 BCE. It regained some prosperity under Venice (1451) but was eclipsed by a pirate raid in 1537. From that time, except for another Venetian interlude, the island remained in Turkish hands until 1826, by which time it was again a modestly successful commercial centre. It was chosen as the temporary capital of independent

Greece (1826–28), but afterward the increasing concentration of business in Athens forced a gradual decay. Today it is a holiday and weekend resort for Athenians, and the ancient pottery trade is still carried on.

Aegina's period of glory was the 5th century BCE, as reflected by the legacy of sculpture and the poetry of Pindar. A well-preserved 5th-century-BCE temple to Aphaea, the ancient Aeginetan deity related to the Cretan Britomartis (Artemis), is situated on a wooded crest in the east of the island. Its Doric peripheral construction (having columns surrounding the building) of local gray limestone has been partially restored.

## Things to Do in Aegina

More travelers come to Aegina (Egina), the largest of the Saronic Gulf islands, than to any of the other Greek islands. Why? Location, location, location. Aegina is so close to Athens that it draws thousands of day-trippers. As the day-trippers arrive in the morning, many of the 10,000 who live on Aegina and commute daily to work in Athens depart. If you have only 1 day for one island, you may decide on Aegina, where you can see a famous temple (the Doric Temple of Aphaia), visit a romantic medieval hill town (Paleochora), have lunch at one of the harborside tavernas in

13

Aegina town, and munch the island's famous pistachio nuts as you sail back to Athens.

A walk along the waterfront of Aegina Town shows off Aegina at its best, giving a glimpse into island life that, despite the presence of Athenian teenagers staring into their iPhones, seems to have never changed over the decades. Fishing boats bob at the docks; a covered fish market, the Psaragora, does a brisk business in the morning; and fishermen hang out on the terraces of ouzeris. A walk inland along winding stone streets to the corner of Thomaidou and Pileos shows off Markelos Tower, a Venetian-era fortified house that in 1827 hosted meetings of the first government in Greece; the pink-and-white landmark now occasionally hosts art exhibits.

Most ships arrive and depart from the main port and capital of Aegina town on the west coast, though a few stop at the resort town of Souvala on the north coast and at the port of Ayia Marina on the east coast. Ayia Marina is charmless, but this port is your best choice, if your principal destination is the Temple of Aphaia.

Despite massive tourism and the rapid development devouring much farmland, the area still has its share of almond, olive, and especially pistachio orchards. In fact, the island has an endemic water problem because of the water necessary for the pistachio groves. Wherever you buy pistachios in Greece, the vendor may assure you that they are from Aegina to indicate their superior quality.

## Best Hotels in Aegina

In addition to the places reviewed, you might consider two other appealing hotels in Aegina town: the Hotel Brown (tel. 22970/22-271), overlooks a sandy beach and is a short walk from the center of town. The stone building is a former sponge factory, converted into a hotel in 1959, and most recently updated in 2008. This stylish 28-room hotel has sea views from front rooms in the main building, its own restaurant, and a cluster of bungalow-like units in its garden; doubles from 75€. If you want a suite with a kitchenette, try the 11-unit Rastoni (tel. 22970/270-39), a 5- to 10-minute hike from the harbor, which has a lovely garden and sea views; many rooms have balconies (from 80€). All these places often have special offers, especially off-season and for long stays.

## Things to See in Aegina

Aegina town's neoclassical buildings date from its brief stint as the first capital of newly independent Greece (1826-28). Most people's first impression of this harbor town, though, is of fishing boats and the small cargo vessels that ply back and forth to the mainland. Have a snack at one of the little restaurants in the fish market (follow your nose!) just off the harbor. This is where the men who catch your snacks of octopus and fried sprats come to eat their catches. The food is usually much better here than the food at the harborfront places catering to tourists.

If you take a horse-drawn carriage or wander the streets back from the port, you'll spot neoclassical buildings, including the Markelos Tower, home of the island cultural center, where there are sometimes exhibits. The Cathedral of Ayios Demetrios, with its square bell towers, is nearby. Carriage ride prices fluctuate wildly, but are usually between 15€ and 25€. In 1827, the first government of independent Greece held sessions both in the tower and at the cathedral. Fans of Nikos Kazantzakis may want to take a cab to Livadi, just north of town, to see the house where he lived when he wrote *Zorba the Greek*. North of the harbor, behind the town beach, and sometimes visible from boats entering the harbor, is the lone worn Doric column that marks the site of the Temple of Apollo (known locally as Kolona), open Tuesday through Sunday from 8:30am to 3pm. The view here is nice, the ruins very ruined. The small museum (tel. 22970/22-637) has finds from the site, notably pottery; it's open Tuesday through Sunday 8:30am to 3pm; combined admission is 3€.

The crumbling remains of the island's longtime capital, Paleochora ★, sprawls across a hillside 5km (3 miles) east of Aegina Town. Abandoned in the early 19th-century when an end to piracy made it safe to settle along the coast again, the ghost town is, quite literally, inhabited by spirits of a sort. More than 30 Byzantine churches remain, and a dozen or so are still in use. Many of these are decorated with faded frescoes, with the best covering the walls of the church of Ayioi Anargyroi. The bus to the beach resort of Ayia Marina makes a stop in Paleochora. If you come here, allow several hours for the excursion.

Lovers of wildlife will want to visit the Wildlife Center and Hospital (ekpaz.gr) in Pachia Rachi. The center is open daily from 9:30am to 7pm and cares for injured and abandoned birds and animals. The Wildlife Center welcomes volunteers as well as visitors.

If you're here in August, you can take some of the 20 or so concerts given by the Aegina Music Festival (tel. 698/131-9332); offerings vary from classical to casual and take place by the Temple of Aphaia, in churches, and on beaches. If you show up in September, you can celebrate Aegina and Greece's most famous nut, the pistachio *(fistiki)*, which has its own festival (aeginafistikifest.gr), usually held on a mid-September weekend.

Culture Calls: If you visit the islands of the Saronic Gulf in July and August, look for posters announcing exhibitions at local museums and galleries. There are often exhibits at the Citronne Gallery (tel. 22980-22-401), on Poros, and at the Koundouriotis Mansion (tel. 22980/52-210), on Hydra. In addition, many Athenian galleries close for parts of July and August, and some have shows on the islands. The Athens Center, 48 Archimidous (tel. 210/701-2268), sometimes stages plays on Spetses and Hydra. The center offers a modern-Greek-language summer program on Spetses in June and July.

**A Swim & a Snack**

One of the island's nicest seaside perches is Perdika, a leisure and fishing port 9km (5 1/2 miles) south of Aegina Town and easily reached via the island bus (see below). Aside from a lively waterfront, with a long line of fish tavernas, the town's sandy beach, Klima, is maybe the island's nicest. For an extra-special getaway, and a refreshing swim, take a boat from the pier in Perdika to Moni, a pine-clad island nature preserve; boats come and go about every hour and charge 5€ round-trip. This is also a good place to have a meal by the sea; Antonis (tel. 22970/61-443) is the best-known and priciest place, but there are lots of other appealing (and cheaper) places nearby. If you visit Aegina with children, you may want to head to Faros (also served by bus from Aegina town) to the Aegina Water Park (tel. 22970/22-540). There are pools, water slides, snack bars, and lots of overexcited children; on hot days, this is a popular destination for Athenian families.

## Temple of Aphaia

Phone 22970/32-398

The Temple of Aphaia commands a promontory facing Athens and the coast of Attica on a pine-covered hill 12km (7 1/2 miles) east of Aegina town. One of the best-preserved and most handsome Greek temples, it's so close to the mainland that both the Parthenon and Temple of Poseidon can be seen on a clear day (with the aid of binoculars); to the ancients, these three sanctuaries constituted a Sacred Triangle. Built in the late 6th or early 5th century B.C., on the site of earlier shrines, Aegina's temple was dedicated to Aphaia, a goddess with the enviable ability to vanish into thin air to avoid unwanted amorous advances.

No one really knows who Aphaia was, although it seems that she was a very old, even prehistoric, goddess who eventually became associated both with Artemis and Athena. According to some legends, Aphaia lived on Crete, where King Minos, usually preoccupied with his labyrinth and Minotaur, fell in love with her. When she fled Crete, he pursued her, and she finally threw herself

19

into the sea off Aegina to escape him. She became entwined in fishing nets and was hauled aboard a boat. A sailor then fell hopelessly in love with the beautiful creature. So she jumped overboard again, swam ashore on Aegina, and, as her smitten admirer watched from his boat, vanished right before his eyes (*afandos* means "disappear").

Thanks to the work of restorers, 25 of the original 32 Doric columns still stand, but the finest feature is missing: a magnificent pediment frieze depicting scenes from the Trojan War. The sculpture was carted off in 1812 by King Ludwig of Bavaria. Whatever you think about the removal of art treasures from their original homes, Ludwig probably did us a favor by taking the sculptures to the Glyptothek in Munich: While he was doing this, locals were busily burning much of the temple to make lime and hacking up other bits to use in building their homes. Still, the setting is so beautiful, you'll hardly miss it.

Allow at least 4 hours for your visit if you come here by the hourly bus from Aegina town; by taxi, you might do a visit in a couple of hours.

## Best Restaurants in Aegina

Remember that fish is priced by the kilogram at most restaurants. The price varies from catch to catch, so it's a good idea to ask before you order. One place where the fish is always fresh is Antonis (tel. 22970/61-443), harborside in Perdika. In Ayia Marina, Kyriakakis (tel. 22970/32-165) has been packing them in since the 1950s; the fish is fresh, the veggie dishes tasty, and the french fries still homemade. If you don't mind being away from the fish and the sea, try Vatsoula (tel. 22970/22-711) in Aegina town; any local can direct you there. Call ahead, as this place with the pleasant garden and tasty spitiko (home) cooking keeps idiosyncratic hours.

## Best Nightlife in Aegina

At sunset, the harbor scene gets livelier as everyone comes out for an evening *volta* (stroll). As always, this year's hot spot may be closed by the next season. As no one answers the phones at these places, we do not list phones. In Aegina town, Avli and Perdikiotika, in another one of Aegina's 19th-century houses, are durable favorites. On summer weekends, En Egina and Kyvrenio have live music and occasional traditional *rembetika* music often from around midnight till dawn. On summer weekends, Armida, a bar/restaurant in a converted caique moored at the harbor, is open from breakfast until, well, breakfast. There are also several outdoor cinemas in town, including the Olympia and the Faneromeni. Young bloods and yachties rub shoulders after dark at the Muzik Bar Café on the Perdika beach. If you want some late-night ouzo and octopus in Aegina town, try Tsias or Pelaisos by the fish market.

## Planning a Trip in Aegina

Getting There
Car ferries and excursion boats to Aegina usually leave from Piraeus's Main Harbor; hydrofoils leave both from the Main Harbor and from Marina Zea Harbor. Hydrofoil service is at least twice as fast as ferries and at least 40% more expensive (except to Aegina, for which the charge is only about 10% more). The sleek little hydrofoils are outfitted like broad aircraft with airline seats, toilets, and a minimum of luggage facilities. (The fore sections offer better views, but they're also bumpier.) The newer Super Cats are bigger, faster, and more comfortable, with food and beverage service. Reservations are vital on weekends. Often, in order to continue to another Saronic Gulf island by hydrofoil, you must return to Piraeus to transfer. Some ferries go from Aegina to the other Saronic Gulf islands. *Warning:* Schedules and even carriers can change, so double-check information you get and then be prepared for last-minute schedule and carrier changes (openseas.gr )is a useful site for ferry schedules as is (gtp.gr).

Daily hydrofoil and ferry service to the Saronic Gulf islands is offered by Hellenic Seaways (tel. 210/419-9200). Saronikos Ferries (tel. 210/417-1190) takes passengers and cars to Aegina, Poros, and Spetses; cars are not allowed to disembark on Hydra. Euroseas (tel. 210/411-3108) has speedy catamaran service from Piraeus to Poros, Hydra, and Spetses. Boats often, but not always, leave from gates E8 and 9 in the main Piraeus harbor. You can usually visit any one of the Saronics for between 20€ and 65€ day-return; the faster the ship, the higher the price. Several cruises offer day trips to Hydra, Poros, and Aegina; for details, see chapter 4, "Cruising the Greek Islands."

For information on schedules for most Argo-Saronic ferries, try one of the numbers of the Piraeus Port Authority (tel. 210/422-6000, 210/410-1480, or 210/410-1441), but phones are not always answered. On Aegina, try tel. 22970/22-328.

Avoiding the Aegina Crowds If Aegina turns out to be too crowded for you, take a short ferry ride to little Angistri, where Rosy's Little Village (tel. 22970/91-610) is as charming as its name, with 16 whitewashed rooms tucked in a pine grove. The restaurant serves organic food, there's swimming in a rocky cove, and many guests meditate and relax, either on their own or in one of a number of holistic workshops; summer doubles start at 50€ and go to around 75€ in August.

Visitor Information
The Aegina Tourist Office (tel. 22970/22-220) is in the Town Hall. There's a string of travel agencies at the harbor, including the usually efficient Aegina Island Holidays, 47 Demokratias (tel. 22970/26-439; fax 22970/26-430). To learn a little about Aegina's history, look for Anne Yannoulis's *Aegina* (Lycabettus Press), usually on sale at Kalezis Boatokshop on the harbor (tel. 22970/25-956), which stocks foreign newspapers..

## Fast Facts in Aegina

The National Bank of Greece is one of four waterfront banks with currency-exchange service and ATMs; some travel agents, including Island Holidays (tel. 22970/23-333), often exchange money both during and after normal bank hours, usually at less favorable rates. The island clinic (tel. 22970/22-251) is on the northeast edge of town; for first aid, dial tel. 22970/22-222. The police (tel. 22970/23-343) and the tourist police (tel. 22970/27-777) share a building on Leonardou Lada, about 200m (656 ft.) inland from the port. The port authority (tel. 22970/22-328) is on the waterfront. The post office is in Plateia Ethatneyersias, around the corner from the hydrofoil pier. The telephone office (OTE) is 5 blocks inland from the port, on Aiakou. There are several Internet cafes, including Prestige and Nesant, on and just off the waterfront. Tip: Try to pick up the useful guides Essential Aegina and Mini Guide, often available from travel agents, hotels, and the tourist police.

## Getting Around in Aegina

A left turn as you disembark the ferry takes you east to the bus station (tel. 22970/22-787) on Plateia Ethneyersias. There's good service to most of the island, with trips every hour in summer to the Temple of Aphaia and Ayia Marina (3€); tickets must be purchased before boarding. Every Saturday and Wednesday in summer, Panoramic Bus Tours (tel. 22970/22-254) offers a 3 1/2-hour bus tour (6€) of the island, taking in the Temple of Aphaia, several beaches and villages, and the Hellenic Wildlife Hospital (tel. 22970/28-267) at Pachia Rachi, where monkeys, wild boar, crocodiles, owls, and other exotic creatures are rehabilitated and housed before being returned to the wild. The tour has a commentary in Greek and English and is a great introduction to the island. Taxis are easy to find in Aegina town; if you want to take a taxi tour of the island, negotiate the fare before you set off. Your hotel can usually get you a decent price to rent either bicycles or mopeds; if you just show up at a rental place, the price is usually higher. An ordinary bike should cost about 12€ per day; mopeds, from 25€, except on summer weekends, when the sky is the limit. Motorcycle and moped agents are required to, but do not always, ask for proof that you are licensed to drive such vehicles and give you a helmet. Be sure to check the tires and brakes.

## Hydra

Hydra, Modern Greek Ídhra, dímos (municipality) and island of the Saronic group in the Aegean Sea, Attika (Modern Greek: Attikí) periféreia (region), central Greece. It lies just off the eastern tip of the Argolís peninsula of the Peloponnese and has a maximum length, northeast-southwest, of 13 miles (21 km). The highest point, Mount Ere, is 1,936 feet (590 metres). Once quite wooded and well watered, as its Turkish name, Çamlıza ("Place of Pines"), shows, it is now denuded and dry, with almost no arable land. Water is collected from rain in cisterns and is also shipped from the mainland.

First prominent in the late 15th century under Turkish rule, it became a seafaring centre. In the 17th century the island received an influx of Albanian refugees from the Peloponnese; maritime trade then thrived. After an abortive insurrection against the Turks in 1770, Hydra received Greek refugees, who also concentrated their energies on commercial shipping. In 1821, at the outbreak of the War of Greek Independence, the island's population had risen to 30,000. With neighbouring Spétsai and Psará islands, the Greeks and Albanians of Hydra placed their considerable merchant fleets and fortunes at the disposal of the insurgents, and Hydriote sea captains commanded Greek ships in several successful encounters with the Turkish fleet.

With the advent of steamships, however, the maritime activities of the island declined. Industries now include sponge fishing, cotton weaving, shipbuilding, and international tourism. Ídhra, the chief town, on the north coast, is an artists' and writers' colony and the residence of a metropolitan bishop. Its narrow, rock-cut streets surround a sheltered harbour. Three other small ports on the north coast are Mandrákion, Mólos, and Panayía. Area 19.2 square miles (49.6 square km). Pop. (2001) municipality, 2,646; (2011) municipality, 1,966.

## Things to Do in Hydra

Hydra is one of a handful of places in Greece that seemingly can't be spoiled. Seafaring merchant families built proud mansions of honey-colored stone on Hydra in the late 18th and early 19th centuries, artists and writers began arriving in the 1960s, and in their wake came the rich and famous and the simply rich. They keep a low profile, however, and with the absence of cars (transport is by foot or mule), Hydra seems wonderfully removed from the modern world. Today, there are often more day-trippers here than "beautiful people," although when elegant Athenians flee their stuffy apartments for their Hydriote hideaway each summer, the harborfront turns into an impromptu fashion show. If you can, arrive in the evening, when most of the day visitors have left, and rejoice in the cool of the evening. Whatever you do, be sure to be on the deck of your ship as you arrive, so you can see Hydra's bleak and steep hills suddenly reveal its perfect horseshoe harbor overlooked by the 18th-century clock tower of the Church of the Dormition. This truly is a place where arrival is half the fun. But the best is yet to be when you step ashore.

Let's start with the cars or, more precisely, their absence. With the exception of a handful of municipal vehicles, there are no cars on Hydra. You'll probably encounter at least one form of local transportation: the donkey. The captains' lasting legacy, their handsome stone *archontika* (mansions) overlooking the harbor, still give Hydra town its distinctive character. (You won't be surprised to learn that the island has been declared a national treasure by the Greek government and the Council of Europe.) The curved, picturesque harbor and these worldly houses overlooking the blue waters (many housing bars and expensive shops), are especially striking because they're enclosed by barren gray and brown mountainsides. The only places on Hydra that are habitable, in fact, are Hydra Town and some small collections of pretty seaside houses at neighboring Kamini and Vuchos, making the island seem even more like a privileged getaway. You'll probably find Hydra town so charming that you'll forgive its one serious flaw: no top-notch beach. Do as the Hydriots do, and swim from the rocks at Spilia and Hydronetta, just beyond the main harbor, or hop on one of the caiques that ply from Hydra town to the relatively quiet island beaches.

## Best Hotels in Hydra

Hydra has a number of small, charming hotels in restored 19th-century buildings. In addition to the following choices, you might try the 19-unit Hotel Greco, Kouloura (tel. 22980/53-200; fax 22980/53-511), in a former fishing-net factory in a quiet neighborhood; the 20-unit Misral Hotel (tel. 22980/52-509), a restored island home off the harbor; or the 27-unit Hotel Leto (tel. 22980/53-385), which is airy and bright, with large bedrooms, a garden courtyard, and one wheelchair-accessible room. If you're traveling with friends, you might investigate the Kiafa, once a 19th-century sea captain's mansion, now a boutique hotel with a pool, in the Historic Hotels of Europe group, that rents to groups of up to nine people (tel. 210/364-0441). In season, doubles start from 75€, with prices considerably higher on weekends and in August.

## Bratsera Hotel
Phone +30-22980-53971 Prices Doubles 140€–240€ with breakfast. Units 25 Amenities Wi-Fi, pool, restaurant, included breakfast, massage, yoga and pilates, meeting and conference facilities

This hotel received an award for its conversion of a 19th-century sea-sponge industry building and we'd say they deserve one for hospitality as well. It retains the traditional Hydriot architecture, with liberal amounts of wood and high ceilings and also has a pool in the courtyard garden beside a wisteria-shaded breakfast area. Rooms can be small, but most of the guests end up spending their time outside, in the serene courtyard, which feels like its a world away from the bustle of Hydra. One final perk: the beds are unusually comfortable, with soft sheets and top–quality mattresses. A real find.

## Cotommatae 1810 Boutique Hotel
Phone 30 2298 053873
In the early 1900's, a band of brothers named the Cotommatae, ship-owners and merchants, criss-crossed the Mediterranean, trading for fine porcelain, European clothing, art objects, luxury furniture and other expensive goods. One of them was named Dimosthenes Kotommatis, and he re-built this house, using

elements of the styles he'd seen during his wanderings to Turkey, the Middle East, Venice and other Mediterranean ports.

Kotommatis' descendents own the guesthouse today, and they've done their best to restore it to its former glory, keeping the burnished chestnut floors and exposed beams, adding new mattresses to the exquisite antique bedframes (one of which is 200 years old) and restoring the painted ceilings in the dining rooom and living areas. To these, and other antique elements, they've added such mod cons as heated towel racks, rainfall showers, Jacuzzis, air-conditioning and fridges in each room.

But despite these contemporary niceties, the history of the house shines through, and its ambiance is old-fashioned, particularly in terms of the gracious hospitality guests receive here. When they arrive, often with their luggage strung across the backs of donkeys (no cars are allowed in Hydra Town), they're offerred cool water and a traditional Hydrian dessert of cherry's in syrup. Breakfast, too, has an air of formality to it, as guests chow down on a wide variety of local treats. A truly special place to stay.

Tip: If you're visiting off-season, or can book many months in advance, don't be shy about asking for a discount. The owners will often rent out rooms at 50% off the rates above when business is slow, and give 15% percent discounts to those who secure their rooms early.

## Hotel Mira Mare
Phone 22980/52300
These bungalows are just yards from the sea on the beach at Mandraki, 1.5km (1 mile) from town (30 minutes on foot, 10 minutes via water taxi).They have standard-issue pine furniture and flagstone floors. The owners have their own boat and run island tours for guests. They also organize beach activities, Greek nights, and other diversions. Open April through September.

## Mistral Hotel
Phone 22980/52509 or 53411
This traditional stone mansion houses elegantly decorated rooms that vary considerably in size. Each room is equipped with a minifridge, and a truly fabulous breakfast is served each morning in the courtyard. Special kudos to the staff, who are wonderfully accommodating and eager to share their knowledge about Hydra with guests. O

## Phaedra Hotel
Phone 22980/53330
All hail Hilda! Sh's the mastermind behind this this charming little hotel, set a former tapestry factory, and her welcome may be the warmest on Hydra. In the morning Hilda and her staff put out a

superb spread of thick Greek yogurts, fresh fruits, home baked goods and more; throughout the day, she's available to answer questions and help with bookings. Not that you're likely to want to stray too far from the hotel.

It's an idyllic place, with views of the hills and the surrounding cobblestone streets, set far enough away from the port to be blissfully quiet. All the rooms are wonderfully spacious, attractive and come with kitchenettes (in order to minimize strong food odors, the hotel discourages guests from cooking full meals); some have two levels, others have patios and there's an interconnecting room for families with two or three children.

## Things to See in Hydra

Summer Festivals in Hydra
On a June weekend often, but not always, the third weekend in June Hydra celebrates the Miaoulia, which honors Hydriot Admiral Miaoulis, who set much of the Turkish fleet on fire in the Battle of Geronta in 1821. The plucky admiral rammed the Turkish fleet with explosives-filled fireboats; casualties on both sides were, understandably, considerable, with more Greek than Turkish ships left afloat. Celebrations include a reenactment of the sinking of a model warship; if you're not on Hydra for the festivities, you may see the fireworks light up the sky from other Saronic islands and the

adjacent Peloponnesian mainland. In early July, Hydra has an annual puppet festival that in recent years has drawn puppeteers from countries as far away as Togo and Brazil. As these two festivals are not on set dates, check for schedules with the Greek National Tourist Office (tel. 210/870-0000) or the Hydra tourist police (tel. 22980/52-205).

## Attractions in Hydra Town

Why did all those "beautiful people" begin to come to Hydra in the '50s and '60s, and why is the island so popular today? As with the hill towns of Italy, the main attraction here is the architecture and setting of the town itself and all the chic shops, restaurants, hotels, and bars that have taken up quarters in the handsome old stone buildings. In the 18th and 19th centuries, ships from Hydra transported cargo around the world and made this island very rich indeed. Like ship captains on the American island of Nantucket, Hydra's ship captains demonstrated their wealth by building the fanciest houses money could buy. The captains' lasting legacy: the handsome stone *archontika* (mansions) overlooking the harbor that give Hydra town its distinctive character. In earlier days, Hydra was a prosperous port that sent ships as far away as America; that history comes to the fore at the harborside Historical Archives and Museum (tel. 22980/52-355; admission 4€; daily 9am–3pm and 7–

8pm), which has old paintings, carved and painted ship figureheads, and costumes. There are sometimes exhibits of work by local artists in a gallery here.

One *archontiko* that you can hardly miss is the Tombazi mansion, which dominates the hill that stands directly across the harbor from the main ferry quay. This is now a branch of the School of Fine Arts, with a hostel for students, and you can usually get a peek inside. Call the mansion (tel. 22980/52-291) or Athens Polytechnic (tel. 210/619-2119), for information about the program or exhibits.

The nearby Ikonomou-Miriklis mansion (also called the Voulgaris) is not open to the public, but the hilltop Koundouriotis mansion, built by an Albanian family who contributed generously to the cause of independence, is now a house museum. The mansion, with period furnishings and costumes, is usually open from April until October, Tuesday to Sunday 10am to 4pm; 4€. If you wander the side streets this side of the harbor, you will see more handsome houses, some of which are being restored into private homes, while others are being converted into boutique hotels.

Hydra's waterfront is a mixed bag, with a number of ho-hum shops selling little of distinction and a handful of jewelry shops and elegant clothing boutiques one bold (or honest) enough to call itself Spoiled! (tel. 22980/52-363). Most of the elegant shops are either on side streets off the harbor, or in the area below the Tombazi mansion. Alas, the wobbly global economy has threatened a number of the nicest shops, and you may not find everything still there when you visit. Elena Votsi (elenavotsi.com) sells her original designs (including a graceful gravity-defying sterling silver clothes hanger for baby's first designer outfit) here and at her shop in Athens's Kolonaki district. Hermes Art Shop (tel. 22980/52-689) has a wide array of jewelry, some good antique reproductions, and a few interesting textiles. Domna Needlepoint (tel. 22980/52-959) has engaging needlepoint rugs and cushion covers, with Greek motifs of dolphins, birds, and flowers. Vangelis Rafalias's Pharmacy is a lovely place to stop in, even if you don't need anything, just to see the jars of remedies from the 19th century.

When you've finished with the waterfront, walk uphill on Iconomou (it's steep) to browse in more shops. Meltemi (tel. 22980/54-138) sells original jewelry (including gorgeous earrings) and ceramics. Just about everything is borderline irresistible especially the winsome blue ceramic fish. Across from Meltemi, Emporium (no phone) shows and sells works by Hydriot and other artists. If you want to take home a painting or a wood or ceramic model of an island boat, try here.

Hydra boasts that it has 365 churches, one for every day of the year. The most impressive, the mid-18th-century Monastery of the Dormition of the Virgin Mary (E Kimisis tis Panagias) is by the clock tower on the harborfront. This is the monastery built of the marble blocks hacked out of the (until then) well-preserved Temple of Poseidon on the island of Poros. The buildings here no longer function as a monastery, and the cells are now municipal offices. The church has rather undistinguished 19th-century frescoes, but the 18th-century marble *iconostasis* (altar screen) is terrific. Like the marble from Poros, this altar screen was "borrowed" from another church and brought here. Seeing it is well worth the suggested donation.

## A Monastery, A Convent & Beaches

If you want to take a vigorous uphill walk (with no shade), head up Miaouli past Kala Pigadia (Good Wells), still the town's best local source of water. A walk of an hour or two, depending on your pace, will bring you to the Convent of Ayia Efpraxia and Monastery of the Prophet Elijah (Profitis Elias). Both have superb views, both are still active, and the nuns sell their hand-woven fabrics. Once you're there, the monks will offer you a glass of cold water in their shady courtyard and probably try to sell you some needlework made by the nuns. They occasionally allow visitors in to see their charming chapel as well. (*Note:* Both nuns and monks observe the midday siesta from 1 to 5pm. Dress appropriately no shorts or tank tops.) Alternately, many visitors make the trip by donkey, with rates starting at a highly negotiable 60€.

Unfortunately, most of Hydra's best beach, at Mandraki, a 20-minute walk east of town, is the private preserve of the Miramare Hotel. If you're on Hydra briefly, your best bet is to swim off the rocks just west of Hydra town at Spilia or Hydronetta, or head out to sandier (and fashionable) Kaminia. Still farther west are the pine-lined coves of Molos, Palamida, and Bisti (all three as sandy as it gets on Hydra), best reached by water taxi from the main harbor (about 10€). The Kallianos Dive Center (kallianosdivingcenter.gr) offers PADI scuba lessons and excursions off Kapari island, near Hydra. Excursion boats from the harbor also set sail for Ayios Nikolaos, a pebble beach with sun beds and refreshment concessions on the south coast (the cost is about 8€ a person round-trip).

The island of Dokos, northwest off the tip of Hydra, an hour's boat ride from town, has a good beach and excellent diving conditions; it was here that Jacques Cousteau found a sunken ship with cargo still aboard, believed to be 3,000 years old. You may want to take a picnic with you, as the taverna here keeps unpredictable hours.

## Best Restaurants in Hydra

The harborside eateries are expensive and mostly not very good, although the views are such that you may not care. The cost of fish, priced by the kilogram at most restaurants, varies from catch to catch, so ask the price before you order. Two longtime favorites off the harbor are still going strong: Manolis (tel. 22890/29-631) and Kyria Sophia (tel. 22980/53-097), both with lots of vegetable dishes, as well as stews and grills. Kyria Sophia's is tiny, so it's vital to try to book a table. A number of cafes also lie along the waterfront, including To Roloi (The Clock), by the clock tower. Omilos (tel. 22980/53-800), by Hydra town's rocky bathing spot, Hydronetta, has terrific salads, with a wide variety of hard-to-find greens and inventive dressings. Out on Kamini beach, Castello (tel.22980/54-101) is open from early to late, serving snacks and full meals to elegantly casual young Athenians who like the mushroom-stuffed hamburgers and foreigners who toy with *mezedes* and Greek salads; there's a resident DJ, a master bartender (apple and pear martinis, anyone?), great views over the sea for sunset or sunrise.

### Sunset Restaurant

Portside, next to the cannons on the cliff over the swimming area
This popular restaurant has a well-deserved reputation for quality and elegant food presentations. It has been around for years, catering to everyone from casual diners to wedding parties. Sunset

serves traditional taverna fare, but most come for the seafood and the romantic, yes, sunset view. Most nights in summer there's live Greek music in summer, and a popular bar.

### Taverna Gitoniko
Honest, home-cooking is the draw here, along with service that will make you feel like you're part of the family. You'll find all the Greek specialties on offer: moussaka, grilled fish, terrific stuffed grape leaves (a house specialty), souvlaki and more. All of this is served in a bric–a–brac laden or on the outdoor terrace, pleasant but nothing fancy. And often, that's just fine.

## Best Nightlife in Hydra
Hydra has an energetic nightlife, with restaurants, bars, and discos going full steam ahead in summer. In theory, bars close at 2am. As always, this year's hot spot may be closed by the next season. Portside, there are plenty of bars. As no one answers the phones at these places, we do not list phones. The Pirate, near the clock tower, is one of the longest living (since the 1970s) and loudest. Veranda (up from the west end of the harbor, near the Hotel Hydra) is a wonderful place to escape the full frenzy of the Hydra harbor scene, sip a glass of wine, and watch the sunset.

Hydronetta tends to play more Western than Greek music although the music at all these places is so loud that it's hard to be sure.

Friends report enjoying drinks at the Amalour, just off the harbor, where they were surrounded by hip, black-clad 30-somethings and listened to jazz, rap, and vintage heavy metal. There are still a few local haunts left around the harbor; you'll be able to recognize them easily. You'll also easily spot the Saronicos; If you don't hear the music, just look for the fishing boat outside the front door.

## Planning a Trip in Hydra

Getting There
Daily hydrofoil and ferry service to Hydra and other Saronic Gulf islands is offered by Hellenic Seaways (tel. 210/419-9200). Saronikos Ferries (tel. 210/417/1190) takes passengers and cars to Aegina, Poros, and Spetses; cars are not allowed to disembark on Hydra. Euroseas (tel. 210/411-3108) has speedy catamaran service from Piraeus to Poros, Hydra, and Spetses. For information on schedules for most Argo-Saronic ferries, try one of the numbers of the Piraeus Port Authority (tel. 210/412/4585, 210/422-6000, or 210/410-1480), but phones are not always answered. On Hydra, try tel. 22980/52-279 is a useful site for ferry schedules.

Reservations are a must in summer and on holiday weekends. *Tip:* Lots of porters, some with and some without mules, meet the boats. If you have enough luggage to require their services, agree on a price beforehand; be prepared to pay at least 14€.

## Fast Facts in Hydra

The National Bank of Greece and Commercial Bank are on the harbor; both have ATMs. Travel agents at the harbor will exchange money from about 9am to 8pm, usually at less favorable rates. The small health clinic is signposted at the harbor; cases requiring complicated treatment are taken by boat or helicopter to the mainland. The police and tourist police (tel. 22980/52-205) share quarters on the second floor at 9 Votsi (signposted at the harbor). The port authority (tel. 22980/53-150) is on the harborside. The post office is just off the harborfront on Ikonomou, the street between the two banks. The telephone office (OTE), across from the police station on Votsi, is open Monday through Saturday from 7:30am to 10pm, Sunday from 8am to 1pm and 5 to 10pm. For Internet access, try HydraNet (tel. 22980/54-150), signposted by the OTE

## Getting Around in Hydra

Walking is the only means of getting around on the island, unless you bring or rent a donkey or a bicycle. Caiques provide water-taxi service to the island's beaches (Bilsi has extensive watersport facilities) and to the little offshore islands of Dokos, Kivotos, and Petasi, as well as to secluded restaurants in the evening; rates run from around 14€ to outrageously steep amounts, depending on destination, time of day, and whether or not business is slow.

# Poros Island

## Poros Today

As You Approach the Island of Poros by boat, the historical clock prevails on the hill's highest peak smothered by prickly pear and pine trees. From here, the view of the port and the coastal areas across is magnificent. Constructed in 1927, it was clearly visible from all angles and is characterized as the main attraction of the city.

It's full of pine trees which reach the shores and the sandy beaches The residents of Poros are no different from other Greek islanders in spontaneity, dignity and hospitality. The large homes on the beach have a neoclassical style in contrast to the common duplex houses in Brinia, Milo, Pounta and Kasteli. The first dwellings were built in 1463 and located around the famous Clock.

In the center of the city you can find the Town Hall, the archaeological museum, a public library along with a reception hall for exhibitions and other cultural events.

Many taverns are sparcely located among the picturesque alleyways and the whitewashed houses of Poros which are surrounded by bougainvillea . Visitors can enjoy souvenir shops, cafeterias, taverns and clubs playing Greek and English music all along the pier.

Along the coast going towards the training center, we come across the **open air movie theater** "Diana" which has premiers of the best films shown this past winter. Right next to it is the exhibition hall of Poros that constantly has exhibitions.

Bus and taxi terminals are located in the center of the beach area. Access to boats that go along the shores of Galata is also available there. Public transportation around the island runs pretty smoothly all day. Buses leave every hour while boats depart every ten minutes. On the beach you can find scooter and bike rentals whereas cars are rented right across the island, in Galata.

Leaving the center, you will see the Pregymnasium in the northwest which happens to be Othona's first residence. Today, this area is used for sailors' training and ranking. After passing the field you will come across a small canal separating Sferia from Kalavria.

After crossing the canal you will encounter Sinikismos, the first community of Asia Minor refugees. Towards the end of Sinikismos, if you follow the spiral road surrounded by enormous pine trees, you will end up in the church of Our Lady Agia Zoni where festivities take place on July 2nd. It's located between a steep cliff with lots of trees and running water where the Temple of Poseidon is also found.

On your way back to the canal's bridge, towards the left and west, you will see an area called Perlia. The road continues along the coast, passes through Villa Galini and Mikro Neorio and, eventually, reaches Megalo Neorio. Further down is the Love cove, the Russian dockyard along with the islet called Daskalio.

On the right hand side of the canal's road you will pass through Kanali. Heading east leads you to Askeli. As you continue, the road branches out towards the monastery of Zoodohos Pygi, going north you will reach the temple of Poseidon, Vagionia and passing by Agio Stathi and Profiti Elia it goes back through Sinikismo to the canal.

## The port of Poros island

The heart of cosmopolitan life beats on the beaches of Poros. Starting from Stavro and reaching up to the west pier of the new harbor of Poros which is 1,020 feet long. Along the pier, the visitor sees plenty of tourist shops, cafes, restaurants, taverns, grill houses, many bars with Greek and foreign music and the local movie theater.

The cultural center, exhibition center, the Chatzopouleios pubic library, the Archaeological Museum, City Hall, all banks and services on the island are also found in the same area.

The starting point for buses and taxis is located in the central beach area. There is access to boats heading towards Galata and the neighbouring coastal area. There is frequent transportation service all day long throughout the island. Buses depart every hour and boats every ten minutes.

On the seaside you will find travel agencies, ticketing offices for ferry and speed boats, three pharmacies, telephone companies, clothing and shoe stores, a supermarket, minimarket, fish market, bike and moped rentals, the press agency, disposable supplies and provisions for boats and whatever other shop you may have in mind.

The beach of Poros, almost all day long, especially at night, is full of life and people strolling on the pier along the sea.

## Architecture of Poros
*The Architectural progress of Poros*

The first period of local folkloric architecture, up to the year 1800, is characterized by stone buildings.

A) Small floor plans, shaped in either elongated rectangles or right angles, adjusted to the bas-relief of the ground. The front side facing the road is narrow yet it has depth, as it follows the land inclination, offering one floor in the front part of the building and two in the rear section.

B) Larger rectangular-shaped floor plans. The dimension of the façade is bigger than its volume. These are the wide frontal buildings where their height and volume is greater than the previous ones. These buildings are called "*kapetaneika*", meaning captains' homes, which is basically an expression of wealth.

These two types of buildings rarely have the same height in the front as in the back. During this period, there are very few buildings used for commercial purposes on the ground floor and residences on the first floor.

**Both narrow and wide frontal buildings have the same structural characteristics:**

- ✓ Trowel plasters
- ✓ Asymmetry of side openings
- ✓ Wooden frames
- ✓ Facing the external wall
- ✓ External glass plates
- ✓ Internal nailed shutters

✓ Wooden balconies with straight, iron rods and light metal guardrails

In the second period (1800-1830), even though the floor plans basically remain the same in having the same proportions, their height seems to be increasing. The construction of three story buildings starts to appear. Their volume is quite impressive.

After the Revolution, especially after the establishment of the Supply Center and the National Fleet's Naval Base, the architectural configuration of Poros is of exceptional importance.

The most important features of the town of Poros during this time are the organized urban growth and the way in which the structure of the socio-economic hierarchy is reflected in the area. This is clearly revealed in the architecture. One can see the aristocratic facades that also grant a folkloric touch.

**The Development Of The Neo-Classical Town**

The first plan to construct sea banks indicated a new era. The beach zone was molded from long artificial mounds of soil and the development of the neo-classical town began. Primarily, it extended along the coast and is distinguished by its urban configuration. Its main feature is the common design having neo-classical elements.

The initial town plan of 1900 was applied to the entire residential area. It involved extensive rebuilding and the widening of roads in the rocky peninsula of Kastelli. Assorted changes gradually led to the deterioration of its picturesque and metropolitan appearance.

There are hardly any differences between the city of the 19th century and the one existing today due to the rocky nature of the land. The white stone houses with the tiled roofs that either extend to the sea or reach the edges of cliffs, with monuments and statues of heroes, such as the one of Kapodistria located at the first Supply Center of the National Fleet (Junior and High School area of Poros), of philhellenes, admirals, etc....

There were, and still are, a numerous amount of buildings known for their architecture, providing elements of the neo-classical design such as: the National Bank, the store "Griva" in St. George, the home of Karras, the first Elementary School, Villa "Galini", etc...

Many other buildings with remarkable structural features shown belong to: Karadimas, Kizonis, N. Samponis, Pagonis, Sp. Vettas, N. Vatikiotis, G. Samponis, Papageorgiou, Korizis (museum), K. Sarantopoulos, Moropoulos, Papaoikonomou, Syxeris, Liamidis, the hotel "Manesi", Koularmanis, Spiros Drouzinas, K. Sampanis and many others.

## Poros of the 50's

During This Period, Poros is even more picturesque and cherished. The enormous shady pine trees spread out up to the coast of the sandy beaches. In the mountainous regions the inhabitants cultivate the olive trees and all sorts of crops whereas on the flatland of "Foussas" there are vineyards, wheat and vetches. The threshing floors of Poros are quite famous. Locust, fig and almond trees are planted on the hillsides.

Many residents breed cattle. At *"Lemonodassos"* (the Lemon Forest) they produce their famous lemon and orange juice. But most natives occupied themselves with fishing and resin collection. By cutting the pine trees, the resign (a sticky flammable organic substance exuded) gathered is initially put in buckets and eventually transferred to large basins. When summer ends, it is carried on horses and mules to Askeli and finally transported by small boats to Peiraia.

The fishermen, as sea experts, did their job according to the equipment and skills which were passed on from their ancestors. Preparing nets, fishing lines, lamps on the shore, slow paddling, grabbing a harpoon and placing the fishing net and twine on the side to have everything handy. Sometimes, when there was no

Coast Guard patrol in sight, they would throw some small explosives in order to get a live catch.

They used boats to transport their products, even in dangerous weather conditions. Gradually, the citizens of Poros started to get involved in tourism. Next to the traditional cafés, the first tourist shops appear selling souvenirs based on folk art.

Many homes transform into guesthouses offering rooms to rent. A vivid image of the homeowners along with the porters waiting for the ship to dock in order to offer hospitality to the island's visitors, guiding them through the whitewashed alleys smothered in jasmine and bougainvillea.

Also, many natives of Poros staffed the island's ships, which gradually begin to increase, while others become boatmen to transfer tourists to the attractive beaches and to go across to Galata. Some of them use their boats even to transport cars from Galata to Poros.

The residents as well as the tourists spent their time at the small cafés and taverns enjoying ouzo and some octopus. Strolling all along the beach was inevitable. They also thought that watching black and white Greek films on the roof terrace of the movie theatre "Diana", engulfed in jasmine, was quite a treat.

There is much interest shown for the festival of the monastery of Zoodochos Pygi on April 19th, the celebrations of the Virgin Mary at the beautiful church in Vrysoula right above Synikismos on July 2nd, Profiti Elia on July 20th, Agia Paraskevi in Foussa on July 26th along with many other festivities honouring different saints.

Finally, we should mention the unique trails through beautifully shaded paths you can enjoy by hiking, riding horses or mules in order to get to the Temple of Poseidon.

In the 50's, people could see various figures roaming the alleyways of Poros such as the door-to-door milkmen who were, actually, two women dressed in black carrying a tin container of milk and selling it around the neighbourhoods.

The street grocers, accompanied by their mules, were selling their products in the alleys. Many peddlers have disappeared today and are greatly missed

## The Monastery

### The Monastery of Zoodohos Pygi

The old historical Holy Monastery of Zoodochos Pigi of Poros is located 4km east of the main city of Poros island and is built on the slope of a pine forest.

It was founded in 1720 a.d. by the Archbishop of Athens Iakovos (Jacob) the 2nd, who, suffering from lithiasis, was miraculously cured, after drinking from the holy water springing near the Holy Monastery.

In 1733 a.d. the Patriarch of Constantinopolis Paisios the 2nd recognises it as a monastery under the Patriarch's jurisdiction. The act gives it a lot of privileges.

Later on, in 1798 a.d., Patriarch Grigorios (Gregory) the 5th, with a sigillion (officially sealed document), which is safely kept in the quest quarters (Archondariki) of the Holy Monastery, ratifies the Patriarch Paisios's the 2nd document, related to the privileges of the Monastery.

*The Monastery's offer (financial, social and spiritual) to the*

*Greek Liberation War in 1821 was invaluable.*

The first Governor of the liberated Greece Ioannis Kapodistrias as well as the great warriors in land and sea Miaoulis, Tompazis, Apostolis, Boudouris, Drosinos, got strenght from their beloved monastery, praying in front of the holy icon of the Mother of God of Zoodochos Pigi monastery.

In 1828, in the establishments of the Holy Monastery, Ioannis Kapodistrias founded the first orphanage of the liberated Greek nation for the orphans of the warriors of the war for freedom. 180 orphans were sheltered in the monastery, which took full care of them.

In 1830, the first Eclesiastical School, in the eastern wing of the Monastery, was founded by I. Kapodistrias, with 15 students. The Governor's vision was to provide the new born state with educated clergymen, willing to work for its spiritual support. The Holy Monastery became a source of spiritual comfort for many believers and other religious people.

In 1814, a group of monks from Mount Athos, called "Kollyvades", took refuge in this Monastery. A few years later, these monks founded the Zoodochos Pigi Monastery at Longovarda in this island of Paros.

In 1821, monks from another monastery of Mount Athos also sought refuge in this monastery in order to keep in safety the sacred and valuable articles of their monastery and the Holy Relic of Saint John the Baptist.

In this monastery also, in the beginning of the 20th century, Saint Nectarios, a saint of our times, stayed for a couple of months as well as other holy ascetic people, who sanctified the place with their prayers and priritual struggles.

## The Main Church (Katholiko)

Katholiko, that is the main church of the monastery, is a bacilica with a dome and a tower like belfry. In both sides of the vestibule of the church there are the tombs of the heroic admirals of the Liberation War of Greece Manolis Tombazis, from Hydra island nad Nikolaos Apostolis, from Psara island.

Inside the church there is an excellent iconostasis (templo) of exquisite craft. It was propably made in Asia Minor, it is five meters high, curved on lime-wood and plated with gold. Its great height and its bending surface towards the main part of the church, help to the excellent acoustics of the building.

On the right of the iconostasis the household icon of Panagia, the Zoodochos Pigi (the life-giving spring), is placed. The old Byzantine icon is dated in 1650 a.d. It is a masterpiece of Byzantine art. Around the main figure of the Mother of God, many miracles that Her Grace worked are depicted.

In front of the icon there is a silver oil lamp, in which a vigil light is burning, as a token of gratitude for the miracle worked by the Mother of God in 1990. After a long period of rainlessness, Panagia listened to the prayers of monks and priests and it rained.

Opposite to the icon of Panagia and on the left of the "templo" there is an icon of the Mother of God painted by the Italian painter and doctor Raphael Tsecoli (1849 a.d.). The icon shows Panagia holding the Holy Infant Jesus and a sceptre. This icon was donated to the Monastery by Tsecoli out of gratitude because his daughter, Archia Tsecoli, who finally died of tuberculosis in 1847, was hosted and cured at the monastery.

Tsecoli has given his daughter's lineaments to the face of Panagia and little Jesus. In the lower part of the icon, Tsecoli painted the Monastery, protected by the Mother of God.

On the left side of the church, near the entrance, there is also a small, miracle-working icon of great value, placed on a wood-engraved stand. It is called Panagia the Amolyntos (Mother of God, the Immaculate), dated in 1590 and is decorated with a gold-and-silver-plated cover. It is called "Evresis", because it was found in the woods. It was offered by monk Zosimas.

On the western wass of the church, the icon of Christ Pantocrator (the All-Mighty God) is hung, made with excellent craftsmanship (1780).

According to tradition, there are two more icons offered by the admirals Basilios Boudouris and Andreas Miaoulis. It is said that

Miaoulis had a gold-and-silver-plated icon of Panagia Zoodochos Pigi with him, in his battle ship "Aris". He had it hung on the ship's bridge and he often prayed in front of it during the sea-lights.

On the outer south wall of the main church a sundial is attached. It is the work of a priest-monk named Galaction Galatis, who was prior of the Monastery.

The Holy Monastery comes under the notice of the Holy Metropolis of Hydra, Spetses, Aegina, Hermionis and Trizinia. It numbers 17 registered monks.

Three of them reside permantely in the Monastery and, apart from their duties as monks, they offer social and spiritual help to the people of the wider territory of the local church.

## Mythology

From antiquity, Poros consists of two isles-Sferia and Kalavria (meaning pleasant breeze), which was initially dedicated to Apollo who then transferred it over to Poseidon in exchange for Delphi.

Kalavria is a larger, very wooded area than Sferia with an abundant water supply. On the other hand, Sferia is basically a cliff formed by some volcanic eruption.

The name "Kalavria" in ancient texts is found in different variations such as "Kalavrea", "Kalavree" and "Kalavreia". It must have gotten its name from a combination of two words- *KALH* (good) and *AVRA* (breeze) which the island has plenty of and originated from the sea across as well as the dense pine forests along with the olive groves of the island.

Another opinion on how the name came up is that Kalavria was named after Kalavro, the son of Poseidon and patron of the island. Prior to the given name, Kalavria, it was also called Irini, Anthi, Yperi, Anthidonia and Skelerdia.

Sferia was named after Pelopa's charioteer, Sfero who had left on his own or was possibly persecuted by Pelopa's servants and was chased all the way to Trizina.

Pelopa's sons, Pithefs and Trizin, reigned there after their father pursued them from Pissa (the city-state near ancient Olympia). Sfero asked for and was granted asylum by them. He was buried in Sferia when he died.

According to Pafsania, goddess Athena, either because Sferos was favored by her or because she wanted to thank Poseidon in some way, appeared in Aethra's dream. Aethra was the daughter of Pitthea, the king of Trizina, and Athena told her (in her dream) to go to Sferia and make a sacrifice on Sfero's tomb. Aethra went to Sferia where she met Poseidon who seduced and slept with her. As for Athena's deception, not only was Aethra not upset, but she built the temple of Apatouria there for her.

From then on, virgins from Trizina visit the temple and dedicate their chastity belts to Athena of Apatouria before they get married. Amazingly, this way, the young women of Trizina were capable of covering any "foolish mistakes" made prior to their wedding. That is the reason why Sferia was called Hiera (Holy).

This legendary shrine was probably situated at Saint George's temple or a little more to the east where an old reservoir is located today. A few remains of this ancient sanctuary can be found in some of Poros' old houses around St. George's church.

## History Mythology

Poros is comprised of two islands Sphairia and Kalavria (the name Kalavria means "gentle Breeze"). Kalavria at first was offered to the god Apollo and he made it over to the god Poseidon in return for Delphi. Kalavria is quite larger than Sphairia and is planted all over. Sphairia is a volcanic rock.

In mythology times Aithra founded in Sphairia the temple of Athena Apatoria in honor of her encounter with the god Poseidon.

In the north part of the island there are the ruins of Poseidon's Temple, which was built in 520BC. The main Temple was built in Doric style, though some of its columns were Ionian. Nearly the Temple there was the built up area of Kalavria.

Such was the place's importance that it functioned as the center for the Amphictyonic League (amphictionnes: dwellers around") a voluntary "cooperative" of city-states in both civic and religious matters, which included Hermione, Epidauros, Aigina, Prassies, Athens and Orhomenos.

At the Poseidon's Temple came Demosthenes the ancient great orator availing himself of its right of sanctuary as Philip the King of Macedonia chased him

In 1821 Poros played a significant role in 1821 Revolution. It was placed on the map of history in 1828 where rival assemblies met to make important decisions, which set the Constitution in a positive direction. In 1830 the building of the shipyard and naval station at Poros began.

## Sightseeings

Viewing the Strait of Poros surrounded by pine, olive, orange and lemon trees. The beauty of the area has been appreciated and praised by prominent writers, poets and artists. Nobel winners such as George Seferis, Kosmas Politis, Kostis Palamas, Julia Dragoumi and the distinguished American writer Henry Miller are some of the island's admirers.

Many of the houses of Poros are samples of neoclassicism. The Deimezi building, made out of gray and red stone, the shop of Grivas, with wide doors and a beautiful interior décor and several others. Villa Galini, though, is considered one of the finest constructions of Poros, built in 1892, which has accommodated famous Art and Literature personalities.

One of the biggest attractions are the neighborhoods of Poros. Tourists and visitors wander among the narrow alleyways of Poros and the white-washed two-story homes in Brinia, Mylos, Punta and Kastelli, full of bougainvillea.

Ascending, after the square of the Town Hall, the picturesque white paves, we reach the small Church of Saint George with small taverns and shops around it. You will be thrilled by the large Platanus that exists in the tavern Platanos, it is 200 years old.

The Archaeological Museum of Poros, located in Korizi Square is open to the public daily from 9.00 to 15.00 except Mondays. Here you will see findings dated from the Mycenaean to the Roman era that arose from the excavations of the Temple of Poseidon, Ancient

Trizina, the Royal Tombs of Magoulas and Apatheia, from Modi and St Konstantinos of Methana. One can even see the magnificent frescoes made by Parthenis in the Cathedral of St. George and visit the Hatzopouleio Public Library.

The conference room of the City of Poros is situated in a historical landmark building designed by a famous German architect, Ernest Chiller. The neoclassical building,renovated in 2002, has a unique artistic quality in detail and can host major conferences for the city, various committees and other private organizations.

The Monastery of Zoodohos Pygi (18th century), built on a green hillside overlooking the sea, is an example of the island's convent architecture. It combines tranquility with simplicity and picturesqueness. At the monastery's entrance there is a fountain which is famous for its healing properties. It was named after the side of a stream, beneath towering trees, over the sea. Founded and built by the Bishop of Athens Jacob II at his own expense along with contributions offered by various residents of Poros.

The church has a basilica style with a dome. It's interior is very impressive with the wooden carved alter (made in Cappadocia, Asia Minor around the 17th century) as well as the Episcopal throne.

The ruins of the Russian Naval Base are found 5 kilometers to the north In 1834, warehouses and bakeries were set up there to refuel and replenish the Russian fleet with supplies while they were sailing in the Aegean Sea. The Russians kept the property until 1900. Since 1989, by decree, the Russian Naval Base was declared a historical landmark, because of its great architectural and historical interest.

Across the Russian Naval Base there is the small island "Daskalio" with its small picturesque Church of the Virgin Mary, on a beautiful cove.

Following the spiral road covered by large pine trees, we arrive at the Chapel of Our Lady of Agia Zoni, which is celebrated on July 2nd. Located between a gorge with lush plane trees and running water. It is one of the most beautiful spots in Poros where many marriages and baptisms take place.

The Diavologefyro is a steep area of wild beauty. located right after the village of Trizina. It's a beautiful cliff with lush plants, full of oleanders, plane and old trees . In the background you will see a small river running The water falls from the mountains creating small lakes in some parts and surrounded by huge rocks. The gorge has walking access , abundant plant life, no trace of civilization and includes many activities like water slides, jumping, etc. Amazingly, there is running water even during summer.

The Lemon Grove (*Lemonodasos*) is a big area full of lemon trees with lots of water and water mills. From the top, the view is panoramic It is basically a forest of over 30,000 lemon and orange trees with scattered taverns all around. Green lemon and orange trees that smell delightfully and provide the perfect setting for romantic strolls.

Situated east of the port is the islet of Bourtzi with its small castle, built in 1827 by the Bavarian philhellene K.Eintek to protect the harbor. Located on the cove of the monastery near the Peloponnesian coast where anyone can swim to visit it. The castle helped the people of Poros detect ships coming from Hydra. Today it is uninhabited

## Poros History

Prehistorical Period ...
The island of Poros, otherwise known as Kalavria, along with the entire southeastern part of the Peloponnese, was inhabited for the first time during prehistoric times.

Throughout that era, the historical years and beyond, Sferia was unoccupied. The only thing that was there was the Temple of Apatouria which was dedicated to goddess Athena.

In the early Hellenic years, the residential area of Kalavria seems quite populated because there is evidence that three settlements existed during this time period. One village replacing the sanctuary of Poseidon's Temple, another in the area which eventually became the town of Kalavria, near the sanctuary and a third one westward, on the mountain slope of Prophet Elijah located further up from the plain of Foussa.

The origin of these residents is basically unknown, but it seems that a couple of them had Egyptian roots just like the first inhabitants of Trizina and all of Argonafplia.

While these pre-Hellenic tribes seem to derive from Egypt, the descent of other tribes later on, such as the Ionians and Dorians, almost completely altered the entire original race but preserved many of their old local traditions.

Chronologically, the area first welcomed Ionian residents, who eventually prevailed and Trizina and Kalavria turned into Ionian cities and had special relations with the inhabitants of Attica and Viotia during that time. This is evident from the worship of Athena of Apatouria since it is typically Ionian. With the descent of the Dorians, Trizina accepted Dorian settlers from Argos, most likely in a peaceful manner

Recently, the discovery of an extended territory (approximately 20 acres) from the early Hellenic period (3rd millenium B.C.), offered us valuable information about prehistoric times.

Specifically, an ancient village of Poros from the early Bronze Age was revealed, at the location of Cape Vasili which is on the northeastern side of the island. This is the oldest settlement ever discovered in Trizina til today. Two well-preserved buildings with large rooms and storage areas came to light.

This settlement is probably associated with the shipwreck that was found a few years ago on the island of Dokos and dated from the same period.

A significant nautical residential area was also observed on the islet of Modi, east of Poros, dated from the last stage of the Mycenaean era (13th century B.C.). The findings indicate that their residents had some type of commercial transactions with other Aegean regions.

## Ancient History

During historical times, Trizinia is Dorian along with Methana and Kalavria. Those days, Trizinia was part of Argos and from there it seems that they accepted the Dorians as their inhabitants.

At the Dorian descent or a little later on, the citizens of Trizinia established the cities of Alikarnassos, Mindos and Theagkela on the southwest coast of Asia Minor.

According to the most prevailing version, the founding of the Amphictiony of Kalavria goes back to the Geometric and Archaic eras. Having the temple of Poseidon as the base in Kalavria, the Amphictionic League is set up as a religious and, in the end, political federation. Ermioni, Epidavros, Aegina, Prasies, Orhomenos and Athens were the seven city members.

Its purpose was to resolve any disputes as well as for commercial transactions. It reached its peak from the last prehistoric years up until the 5th century B.C.

Later on, inhabitants of Kalavria along with the cities that form the Amphictiony create Sibari located in southern Italy, offering the name Kalavria throughout its neighboring area taken from the Amphictiony of Kalavria.

That is how the residents of Trizinia and Kalavria turned out to be the founders of Alikarnasos, Mindos and Theagkela in Asia Minor, Sibari and the surrounding area of Kalavria in southern Italy along with the municipalities of Sfittos, Anaflistos and Pithaes in Attica.

## Poros During The Vyzantine Era

Kalavria along with Trizina still existed throughout the early Byzantine years as part of the province of the Byzantine Empire.

But Alaric, leader of the Visigoths, who had settled on the north side of the Balkan peninsula from the beginning of the 3rd century, went across Thessaly and reached central Greece from Thermopylae. The Goths arrived in Attica and Boeotia destroying everything in their way. From the entire destruction, Athens was the only city that pulled through. Corinth, Sparta, Argos and Trizinia got looted by the Goths. They caused such great damage in the region that from the last disastrous invasion, around the last months of 396 A.D., Trizinia and Kalavria ceased to exist.

A few years after the destruction of southern Greece by the Goths of Alaric, a great earthquake literally destroyed what was left of the vicious fury of the Goths. Around that time, Vagionia (a settlement in Kalavria) must have sunk in the sea. The rubble of houses and streets of the city are quite apparent in the shallow waters of the Gulf of Vagionia.

After these regional disasters, while Trizina managed to establish the settlement of Damalasin the succeeding Byzantine years, Poros failed to develop any significant village or residential area. Pirates during the Byzantine years and under Ottoman rule literally plagued the area and used the Vagionian bay which even today is called Barbaria.

At that time, Sfera was uninhabited while Kalavria had a few people who lived in isolated farmhouses and were engaged in the cultivation of a couple of farms and livestock.

## Franks Domination

On April 13th 1204, the Crusaders managed to conquer Constantinople with their Fourth Crusade.

The outcome of this conquest was to share the Byzantine Empire amongst the crusaders' leaders according to the feudal system which existed at that time in the West. Thus various Latin states were founded such as the Achaic domination, the estates of Athens and of the Aegean along with several other small states.

Virtually the entire Peloponnese fell into the hands of the Achaic authority, led by Prince William. After him, Godefreigo Villardouino was in control.

Poros and Trizinia, along with the entire area of Nafplio and Argos, belonged to the supremacy of Achaia. But in 1212 the region was ruled by the Duke of Athens where Otto Delaros, the son of a nobleman from Burgundy, was proclaimed the leader.

Throughout Frankish rule, Poros was practically deserted and Barberini pirates held their base on the northern coast.

During the Venetian dominance, Damalas was the baron of Damalet and at the time of Pope Inokentios the 3rd, he became a Latin bishop. The archdiocese was maintained until the area was occupied by the Turks.

## Turkish Domination
*The Turks In Poros ...*
... on March 29th 1453, Constantinople and just about all of Greece as well were occupied by the Turks until 1460, except for some areas that were taken over by the Venetians.

Sferia became populated around 1460. Its first inhabitants were Arvanites who came from the Peloponnese chased by the army of Sultan Mohammed II the Conqueror and the Great Vizier Mahmoud, and thus created the island's first settlement, Kastelli, around the well-known Clock today. They preferred this location because it could serve as a fortress which would protect the residents from the Algerian pirates. Many names of places that have been maintained in Sferia and especially in Kalavria are of Arvanite origin.

The beach, from Punta until the pregymnasium, was inhabited for the first time after 1800.

Since 1688 and throughout the fifteen year duration of the Venetian-Turkish war, Poros was the base for the Venetian admiral Morozini, who used the island as a naval station for his fleet. This was where he heard the news about him being declared Doge of Venice (July 1688).

Around 1700, many Greeks went to Hydra and Poros due to pressure from the Turks. This caused the spreading of the Greek language to these islands, which until then had only spoken the Arvanite dialect.

The second colonization of the island which is made in 1715 by Arvanites again, who faced the wrath of the Turks because they had collaborated with the Venetians. Over the years Arvanites and Greeks created a new society free from hatred and conflicts, with a common national awareness and orthodox religion.

The island came under Turkish occupation in 1718 with the Treaty of Passarowitz, finally banishing the Venetians for good. Since then, Poros was under the leadership of Kapoudan Pasha, always accompanied by a governor.

During the Rebellion of 1770 (Orlov) Alexis Orloff had set up his admiralty on the island.

In 1806, Russia and Turkey come to war again. At that time, the Russians make the naval station at Poros whose ruins still exist in an area a bit after Neorio.

In the years before the declaration of the Revolution, in 1813, Poros, Hydra as well as the other islands, confronted the big problem of inaction (naval crisis) due to the problems encountered in trade and shipping at the time. The Napoleonic wars had ended. The Mediterranean maritime trade fell in the hands of the French and British once again, while ships remained on the island's ports.

Poros had acquired the presence of a governor on the island and simultaneously had repeatedly tried to create a Greek school. These testimonies come from our Epiphanios Dimitriadis, who was invited to teach at Poros (1788-89), and Nikiforos Pamboukis who taught on the island in 1812-13.

During 1819 and 1820 commercial trade recorded its steepest plunge mainly for Hydra and Spetses, where the residents had large ships traveling across the Mediterranean, even in the Black Sea, while the ones that belonged to the residents of Poros were smaller and traveled shorter distances, thus the impact of the crisis on them was much less.

Poros 1821 ...

Poros played a vital role in the Revolution of 1821, the time period when many monuments were preserved.

In August of 1818, Anagnostaras and Elias Chrysopathis came to Poros and Hydra as emissaries of the Filiki Etairia (Society of Friends).

This was where Nikiforos Pampoukis, a monk and teacher, was initiated. Afterwards, the merchants and captains of ships followed in the initiation as opposed to the elders who were cautious about it. Nikolaos Pampoukis was referred to as a catechist in the Filiki Etairia of Hadjianastasi Manesis and Kyriako Douzinas. The number of residents of Poros that were initiated in the Filiki Etairia was remarkable.

On the eve of the riots, all three islands (Poros, Spetses and Hydra) had men who were not only skilled warriors but also had a strong bond amongst themselves.

This helped in manning the warships with men from all three islands, especially from Poros. One thing that must be taken into consideration is the fact that a large number of ships from Hydra and Spetses had a wintry anchorage in Poros because their ports were small.

Notable skippers along with common people, either as officers, commanders-in-chief, sailors or soldiers were found at the fortress from the first moment. Their mission on land begins with the declaration of the War and from April of 1821, they vigorously participate in the Greek Revolution.

Thus, the revolutionary flag of Poros is raised and the residents armed with rifles in their hands begin, enthusiastically, to carry out the dream of many generations. By then, Poros had already been an informal dockyard of the rebellious nation.

Besides the vessels and the manned fleet (officers, commanders or boatmen), extra technicians and necessary materials were offered for the war.

Most people from Poros, depending on their capabilities, provided weapons for the soldiers and campaigned in the siege of Corinth and Akrocorinth in April and May of 1821 accompanied by the residents of Aegina and Dervenohoria and continued throughout the war.

The skippers offered their ships (Manesis, Kapasakis, Nitis, Vesis, Kofinas, Karamanis and others), the merchants offered their money and everyone participated in the financial enhancement of the Supreme Administration handing over 3,600 gros (Medieval coinage) from charity work done throughout the Aegean islands, as stated in a document dated August 22nd 1823 by the elders of the town. The donation of 262,686 grosses offered by the people of Poros up until the 23rd of December 1823 was revealed in another document. Therefore, without any hesitation or ulterior motives, they serve their country intending to be freed from the Turkish rule.

It is well known that during the Greek Revolution of 1821, Hydra played a major role in the nation's naval battle.

The supplies necessary for the Marines were kept there but in February of 1827, they were transferred to Poros because the residents of Hydra persistently tried to seize them. Consequently, a basic naval station was set up. Weapons, guns, bullets, ropes, sails, anchors and pulleys were placed there, whereas health and pharmaceutical supplies came directly from Marseilles.

There, the Maritime Committee in February of 1827 rented warehouses and chartered a fishing boat to transport the provisions from Hydra because the Turkish fleet had set sail and was expected to attack Hydra and Spetses.

Their main concern was Hydra being looted. So, from then on, Poros becomes an informal yet essential naval station for the free Hellenic nation. The Relief Committee will also be established there

(Heideck, Baily and a Greek banker named Ksenos who was Goss' assistant).

Poros built central warehouses where supplies from foreign philhellenic committees were arriving, mostly American, to be distributed to famished civilians and Greeks who were suffering. The first shipment arrives from America to Poros on May 19th , 1827 and is unloaded after Miaoulis and Kanaris accepted it. More than eight supply shipments came from America after that.

The allied fleet started from Paros in the victorious battle of Navarino in 1827.

In June of 1827, J. Miller (the first American philhellene) came to Poros accompanied by his compatriot, Henry Post as representatives of the New York Philhellenic Committee. Their mission was to distribute relief supplies.

At that time, Poros was accommodating dozens of refugees. On November 25th in 1827, the first Naval Hospital was inaugurated by the Bishop of Damalas, Jonah from Trizinia which was constructed by American compatriots S. Howe, Russ and J. Miller.

Poros was not only considered the safest harbor but the most secure and peaceful place. The committee of the 3rd National Assembly held its meeting in Nafplio on August 2nd 1826. Even though publication #122 was unacceptable, it states that Poros is considered the ideal place to hold meetings because it was safe and free from massive crowds, which therefore made it easier for the committee to carry out its work faster

The anti-governmental committee became well known by the Assembly of Trizina in April 1827. It classified Poros as its headquarters on April 15th 1827, where it remained until June 16th, 1827 and temporarily had power until the arrival of I. Kapodistrias in Greece. A conference of ambassadors of the Three Defending Powers was held here that autumn as well.

In October 1828, the meeting of the three Powers took place in Poros, so as to define the borders of the newly established Greek state.

In 1830, the first military naval dockyard of independent Greece was built at the port of Poros

Specially important historical events were occuring in Poros in 1831 during the strong civil conflict between I. Kapodistrias and the residents of Hydra, which resulted in blowing up a part of the Greek fleet that was anchored in the bay of Poros.

## Antiquities of Poros island

*The Temple Of Poseidon ...*

It has been confirmed that the archaeological area round the sanctuary of Poseidon has been inhabited since the Prehistoric times, while probably the sanctuary existed since the Geometrical ones. All the tenements were completed in different time phases. Especially the building of the Sanctuary dates at the Archaic era - and does not seem to have sustained any changes afterwards. The formation of the sanctuary with a row of buildings, the oldest of which were built in 420 b.C. and the newest ones in 320 b.C., is dated at the Classic era. The relics of the town have reference to the Hellenistic era, whereas all seem to survive in Romaic one.

The Sancuary of Poseidon was built somewhere round 520 b.C. We do not know whether there was an older sanctuary. Its dimensions were 14,40 x 27.40 m. facing to the northwestern and it was doric, with 6 columns at the narrow and 12 at the long sides. It must have had internal colonnades, also doric. It was built by aeginian sinter.

The Sanctuary was found in a rectangular parvis, with dimensions 52,95 x 26,05 m. It had two entrances, one to the northeastern side, right opposite of the temple entrance, and a second one to the southeastern side, in the middle of the corresponding side of the sanctuary.

As far as the classic era is regarded, the only extra thing that we are aware of is the creation of a wider sacred precinct at the southeastern of the old one and an extention to the southwestern.

At the northwestern side of that extention, somewhere round 420 B.C., an archway was built, facing to the southeastern. Its dimensions were 9, 30 x 30, 20 m., probably 9 Doric pillars to the front and 4 Ionic at the central long pivot.

50 years later a new archway was built, to the southwestern of the previous archway, few relics of which were saved. Its dimensions were 30, 50 x 9, 45 m. and had 5 internal pillars.

20 years later opposite of it a new archway was built, facing to the northwestern side (dimensions 29, 65 x 7, 40 m.).

At the first Hellenistic years the constructive program of the sanctuary is continued and completed. Between the second and third archway a complex is built that contains the living quarters of the priests and at the southeastern a propylon H shaped with archways to the front and back, with a total lenght of 13, 80 m and width of 6,90m.

About ten years after the propylon, somewhere around 320 B.C. a new archway was built (32, 80 x 3, 95 m.) at the extention of the third one, with Doric collonade.

It is one of the three biggest sanctuaries of Poseidon in Saronicos. The sanctuary shaped isosceles triangular with the sanctuaries of Afaia in Aegina and Poseidon of Sounio. It is found at the location Palatia, between Vigla and Prophet Helias.

The building construction at the southwestern side of the sanctuary (dimensions 31 X 11m.), might have been the Parliament of the town of Kalavreia. That was the meeting place for the delegates of the seven towns that participated in Amphictyony of Kalavreia. At the southwestern side of the Parliament there was a building (Demosthenis' monument or the Aesculapion).

The sanctuary was a famous shelter that accepted under its protection the hunted people. We know the name one of the implorers: Demosthenis. Demosthenis, the orator, was the most famous person who asked for shelter here, leaving Athens, which was occupied by the Macedons. It was here that he drank the poison and was burried in the sanctuary. The Sanctuary was also known at the antiquity for its role as capital of a religious association, Amphiktiony of Kalavreia. The sanctuary of Poseidon was served by many priests and always by a virgin priestess who, after her marriage, was replaced by another virgin.

In 50 BC the sanctuary was plundered by Cilician pirates, around 396 AD by the Goths and what remained was destroyed by the earthquakes as well as by the hands of ulteriors.

In 1774 a lot of porous and other processed stones were transfered to the bay of Vagionia and from there to Hydra for the reconstruction of the church of Virgin Mary.

Today, only a few foundations are rescued along with some plates with inscriptions on them to reveal the magnificence of the ancient sanctuary.

The whole area has been characterised as an archaeological site. Excavations were done for the first time at the sanctuary of Poseidon in 1894 by two Swedish archaeologists and continue until now.


## Colonization of Poros island

*Arvanites*
Colonies here, as in Hydra and Spetses, were established by ancestors of Arvanites, under the pressure of historical events which caused the downfall and their settlement on the Hellenic Peninsula as well as the Peloponnese from 1320 up until the end of the 15th century, their assimilation from Greek principles and,

eventually, seeking refuge in the islands of Argolida. The Arvanites initially came to the area of Argonafplia from ancient Illyria.

*Nerios Atzayiolis* in 1384, *Emmanuel Kantakouzinos* in 1350 and *Theodore Paleologos* in 1405 brought these people to the Peloponnese in order to increase the population there after the destruction caused by invasions.

Due to the fact that the Arvanites fought against the Turks, they were chased with rage by them. Especially Mohammed the conqueror, after his victory in the Peloponnese in 1459 and 1460, gave orders to kill them. So, because the Arvanites who resided around Nafplio were being fiercely chased by the Turks, they were forced to move to the utmost distant coasts of Argolida and occupy the neighboring islands- Poros, Hydra and Spetses.

A group of these Arvanites found shelter in Sferia and built their first homes in Kasteli, around the landmark of the historical clock. They preferred this area because they perceived it as a fortress and supposedly protected them from Algerian pirates, who during this era, invaded, robbed and literally plagued all of Greece.

The second colony on the island is established in 1715, once again by Arvanites, who faced the wrath of the Turks because they collaberated with the Venetians.

This settlement completed the residential view of Poros. Over the years, Arvanites and Greeks created a new society free from hatred and tension, sharing the same national ideology as well as the orthodox religion.

Later on, when there were more inhabitants, and the dangers caused by pirates diminished, the settlements of Brinia, Pounta and Mylos were built a little further from the coast. The beach became a residential area for the first time in 1800 from Pounta up to the Progymnasium.

Today's indigenous residents of Poros are descendants of this group of Arvanites who came and settled first in Sferia. However this should not disappoint today's natives because the ancient Illyrians, otherwise known as today's Arvanites, have a common background with Greeks and, essentially, are of the same origin.

Besides Illyrians were the Byzantine Emperor Justinian and Olympiada, the mother of Alexander the Great. Also, Admiral Kountouriotis, most naval fighters in 1821, from Hydra and Spetses, including the Souliotes of Marko Botsari and Kitso Tzavella were descendants of Arvanites as well.

But many names of places where the residents of Sferia and especially Kalavria have settled come from Arvanite origin. Near

Mylos is a place called "Cro" which means water source in the Arvanite language.

Words like Brinia and Pounta have an Arvanite descent. The same stands for certain surnames that one comes across today in Poros. Names such as Priftis (priest), Kolias (Nicholas), Gikas (harmless), Gionis (world), Ginis (silver), Laskos (Lascaris), and those that are pure Greek but from Arvanite descent, like Triantafyllou, Economou, Papaioannou, Moraitis, Maniatis, Sotiriou, Koryzis, Vetas, Tsamis, Agalou, Logothetis, Antoniou, Anastasiou.

In Kalavria, Arvanite names of places have remained and are as follows: Cape "Achedo" said Bisti (tail), Skarpeza (place with dry wood), Cro (water source), Kontita (watering animals), Modi (louse), also Tselevinia was named this way because the cape is guarded by Arvanites with their boats and whenever Turkish vessels were in sight, they would notify the others who were ready to attack by shouting "tselyeh" (beware), "venyeh" (their coming), tselyeh-venyeh which eventually became today's Tselevinia.

## Cretans

During the Cretan Revolution (1866-1869), families of Cretan fighters fled to Poros in search of , hospitality and medical care. It was a difficult historical circumstance, where thousands of heroic

Cretan warriors and civilians (women, children, elders, clergymen and monks) got killed and the rest of the residents of Crete suffered the consequences. In this framework, many islanders were forced by horrible circumstances to migrate and seek refuge in various Aegean islands.

Thus, more than 500 Cretans fled to Poros, unable to withstand the fury, the rage, the humiliation, the daily persecution and disgrace on the part of the Turks.

The residents of Poros responded cordially. Trizina's Mayor, John Drosinos, tended to unite the residents in a campaign of love for fellow refugees. He, as a doctor, was once the Chairman of the local " Cretan Refugee Relief Committee " and worked vigorously to recover their health, since many of them suffered physically and mentally because of their suffering, deprivation, mental anguish, longing for their families and being very concerned about the future.

Medical care, financial aid, food and hospitality were offered. Even a substantial amount of money was gathered and sent out to the "Cretan General Commission" in Athens.

The love and compassion throughout the island for the refugees and especially Mayor Drosinos' behavior provoked feelings of gratitude to the unfortunate Cretans, exemplified by writings of the time, signed by them.

Most of the refugees came from Rethymno, an area which suffered immensely throughout the Cretan Revolution.

From historical documents of that time, we can identify the names of Cretan families who fled to the island of Poros and till today have been residing there. Surnames such as Perasakis, Palierakis, Alexandrakis, Yannakoudakis, Stagakis, Aretakis, Klados, Kourmoulakis, Spithouris, Faroudakis, Kanellakis and many others.

## Archeological Museum

The Archaeological Museum of Poros is located at the Korizi square. It was created thanks to a pioneer devotee of archaeology, who carried out by himself the hard work of preserving the ancient findings of Trizinia, Christos Fourniades. Fourniades started to collect, by his own initiative, the scattered ancient findings of the area and gather them at the Municipal Office of Poros. In 1958 Fourniades, supported by the Municipal Council of Poros, had already proceeded with the foundation of an Archaeological Collection on the island.

The "Museum of Poros" was lodged temporarily at the old house of Korizi, which was donated in 1962 by the inheritors of Alexandros

Korizis to the Greek State and was demolished in order for the Museum to be built. The Collection of Poros is officially recorded for the first time in 1959.

The Museum of Poros, built during 1966-1968 on the ruins of demolished residence of Korizi, for ten whole years was a shut store house. A first exhibition of the antiquities, limited at the ground floor, was conducted in 1978. Because of the abundance of the findings revealed at the excavations during the last twenty years, the necessity for a new exhibition layout on the ground floor and its expansion to the upper floor came out, works that were acted out in 1998 and gave the Museum of Poros the shape it has today.

The exhibition of the museum covers two rooms, one on the basement and one on the building's floor and includes exhibits from all over the territory o Trizinia and some of the area of Ermioni.

The museum has sculptures, inscriptions and architectural parts from Trizina, Kalavreia and Methana. The most important exhibits are a big anaglyph with a dog's representation on, which was built-in on an ancient construction, a plaster cast of the known inscribed column from Trizina with the script of the Athenean voting, suggested by Themistocles in 480 BC, regarding the encounter of the Persian invasion, an archaic inscription (around 600 BC) from a funeral mark found in Methana, an honourable voting of Trizina

(369 BC) and the inscribed pedestal from a copper statue of the emperor of Rome Marcus Aurelius, offering by the town of Methana (175 180 AD).

Two statuettes, a nude boy and a woman with pallium and cloth, a statuette of Asklipios from Kalavreia, and a few tomb steles of the 4th century BC., from the cemetery areas of the ancient town (such as a remarkable tomb anaglyph with a woman's presentation in hyperphysical size), are some of the most important exhibitions of the classic period.

As far as the imperial period is regarded, during which a series of imposing tomb monuments were made round the town walls, tomb steles of Trizina are exposed such as the tomb stele of Xenokratis orator from Kalavreia (3rd cent. BC).

Furthermore, also exhibited at the museum is a series of capitals of the three main architectonic rhythms from the archaic to the Romaic years: one Doric of the 6th cent. BC, another Doric as well, of the 5th cent. BC. and an angular ionic of the 4th cent. BC that is completed with two examples of Corinthian capitals of the Romaic period, one from Methana and the other from Trizina. The second one is decorated on its main sides with anaglyph visards, testifying that it comes from a theatrical construction.

Finally, samples of old-Christian architecture, such as capitals of that period from the wider area of Trizina, constitute important part of the exhibition

## Why In Poros

## Activities

Poros, the island of peace, romance and entertainment, with pine trees reaching the rugged shores and sandy beaches, with its intense nightlife, also offers its guests activities , for unforgettable vacations.

First of all, it's worth taking a walk around the port of Poros island, while visiting the quaint small shops, that sell everything from local products to clothes, sitting on the front beach and on the paved streets above it.

Visit the Archaeological Museum of Poros with exhibits of findings from the excavations of the Temple of Poseidon, Ancient Troezen, the Royal Tombs of Magoula and other antiquities from Trizinia place.

Continuing on you can take a walk to the Historical Clock Tower of Poros which dominates the highest peak of the hill, amongst pine trees and prickly pears. From there the view of the harbor and the opposite coast is excellent.

After Sinikismos location and following the winding road that follows, you can visit the small Chapel dedicated to the Virgin Mary, located in a beautiful ravine with platanus trees and running waters.

Continuing the same road, after the small Chapel, you pass the "Paradisos Tavern", an ideal place for weddings and chistenings, and continuing you meet the beach "Vagionia", and following the coastal road you will meet the location Palatia, where is the Temple of Poseidon and the place where the ancient orator Demosthenes drunk the poison. From this Doric Temple (6th century) today remains only minimal findings.

It's worth to visit the Monastery of Zoodochos Pigi (18th century), built on a green slope, depicting an example of the islanders monastery architecture, combining tranquility with simplicity and charm.

After Gefiraki place, located in Progimnastirio location, continuing left you will reach the Russian Dockyard, designated as a historical monument due to its great architectural and historical interest.

## Daily excursions
### A. By car

1. Poros - Methana (Loutropolis of Methana 22,1 klm - 30 minutes)

From Galata and following the road toward Athens, at the location Agioi Anargiroi, at the intersection turn right to reach Methana, a coastal spa town with its volcano and spring water sourches.

Methana is a touristic area ideal for family and alternative tourism. Is a romantic destination where you will see the simplicity and the connection with nature. It is ideal for those who seek true relaxation and desire to explore hiking trails and archaeological findings.

2. Poros - Vathi (Vathi Methanon 22,2 klm - 30 minutes)

From Galata and following the road toward Athens, at the location Agioi Anargiroi, at the intersection turn right to reach Methana. After taktikoupoli town, at the left there is a coastal road that leads to the fishing village of Vathi with fish taverns and a beautiful beach to swim.

Vathi is a small fishing village at the bay of Epidavros. It is an ideal destination for relaxing vacations, an oasis of tranquility just under the volcano of Methana.

3. Poros - Nafplio (Nafplio 71,6 klm - 1 hour and 15 minutes)

From Galata and following the road toward Athens, after the old Epidavros we turn left and reach Nafplio, one of the most picturesque towns of Greece, which has been characterised as a traditional settlement.

4. Poros - Mycanae (Mycanae 89,3 klm - 1 hour and 30 minutes)

From Galata and following the road toward Athens, after the old Epidavros we turn left and reach Nafplio. We follow the sign which writes Mycanae and you reach one of the most historical settlements of Greece. Mycanae was an ancient town of Argolida close to the mountain Tritos and opposite the Argolic Gulf.

5. Poros - Ancient theatre of Epidavros and Epidavros beach
( Ancient theatre of Epidavros 49,2 klm - 55 minutes and Epidavros beach 46 klm - 45 minutes)
From Galata and following the road toward Athens, after the old Epidavros we continue left towards Ligourio and then we reach the ancient theater of Epidavros where during the summer months they have gor theatrical plays. After the old Epidavros we turn right and we reach the Epidavros beach.

6. Poros - Metochi - Hydra (Metochi-Hydra 25,1 klm - 40 minutes)
45 minutes from Galata, following the coastal road we reach Metochi, a coastal area opposite of Hydra island, where there is a secure parking for your car.

7. Poros - Hermioni (Hermioni 40 klm - 55 minutes)

55 minutes from Galata, following the coastal road we reach Metochi and we continue to the coastal location of Hermioni.

8. Poros - Kosta - Spetses (Kosta-Spetses 59,5 klm - 1 hour and 15' minutes)

1 hour and 55 minutes from Galata, following the coastal road we reach Metochi and we continue to the coastal location of Hermioni. Then we continue to Kosta, opposite to Spetses island and with a secure parking to leave your car.

9. Poros - Porto Cheli (Porto Cheli 55 klm - 1 hour and 10' minutes)

1 hour and 55 minutes from Galata, following the coastal road we reach Metochi and Hermioni and then the picturesque Porto Cheli.

B. By flying dolphin or flying cat

You can go by flying dolphin or flying cat from Poros to Hydra, Spetses island, Porto Cheli and Hermioni and so Poros island is offered for daily trips to those islands.

C. By ferry boat

You can go by ferry boat from Poros island to Aegina island and so Poros island is offered for daily trips to this island. If you go for more than one day then you can go to the close island of Agistri.

## Water sports

In the beautiful evergreen island of Poros, the "lagoon" along with very good weather conditions and mild winds create a superb training center which is a perfect area for sports and other activities. It has great infrastructure, facilities, schools and clubs for learning and training. You will find any water sport you have heard about or ever imagined and the appropriate qualified instructor to train you.

In Poros there are two water sports schools, Askeli and Neorio, where you will fill your days with fantastic fun activities such as windsurfing, water skiing, wakeboard, jet-ski, banana-boat, tubes, parasailing etc.

You will find a water ski school in Neorio where beginners can indulge in this sport with the help of experienced trainers.

In Poros you can get involved in rowing, kayaking and sailing at the two water sports clubs located on the island.

The rocky sea bottom on the north side of the island, especially in the peninsula of Cape Aherdo and its two sheltered coves, is the ultimate spot for snorkeling.

## Trekking

Discovering the paths through the untouched natural environment, smelling the scent of pine everywhere and admiring the fascinating view of the surrounding area from the hills of the island will be a great reward for those who choose to do it.

Trizinia...
Poros and generally the province of Trizinia is one of the few areas that have a wide variety of interests to offer which would be unfair to our island as well as to thousands of Greek and foreign visitors to remain inaccessible.

Environment ...

The modern visitor is searching for something more than soaking up some sun or other forms of entertainment.

Today, being more mature, more educated, and sensitive to environmental issues, history and culture he explores and learns everything about an area inside out.

Escape...
Searching for an alternative way to escape. A hiking excursion to places of historical, geological and naturalist interest, through paths to the unfamiliar side of our island.

Until the 60's, the road went up to the Monastery towards the right side of Kanali and up to the left part of Neorio.

Locals and tourists went to various locations of Poros on foot or on horseback through the beautiful trails, many of which are preserved until today.

The path started from Sinikismos, passed through the fountains of Virgin Mary, continued to Profiti Elia, then to Saint Stathis and finally ended up at the Temple of Poseidon.

Another way to go to Poseidon's Temple was from the Monastery through the residential area of "Samouili".

From the Temple one could go down to Vagionia to go swimming through Foussa or go fishing in Skarpiza passing by "Cro", a beautiful estate with running water.

Across, in Galata, tourists started from Plaka with donkeys to visit the famous Lemon Forest, with its watermills and waterfall which help maintain the green lemon trees.

Another route was the one that started from the village of Trizina, across to Galata and passed through the boulder of Theseus to end up in the Diavologefyro.

**Sports**

Along with fantastic weather conditions and mild winds provide a magnificent training center, which is the ideal place for nautical sports activities.

The main reason for highly developed water sports in Poros is because it provides great infrastructure, facilities, schools and clubs for learning and training.

Rowing competitions are held annually in Poros in which many organizations took part from different areas, therefore, making it a special event. Various prominent Greek and foreign oarsmen have trained in Poros.

There are two nautical associations, N.O.P.T. and ONAT, and two water ski schools in Neorio and Askeli.

*From N.O.P.T., Dimitri Mougios became a Silver medalist in the rowing competition in the 2008 Beijing Olympics*

**N.O.P.T.**

N.O.P.T. founded in 1971 and operates in Poros and the region of troizina. N.O.P.T. operates segments of rowing, canoeing, water ski and dancing school.

NOPT trains about 90 athletes in all departments and enhance almost every year the national rowing teams, canoe-kayak and water ski.

The rowing athlets of the 1983 participated for the first time in National Games with a small group and then slowly built, arriving in 1996 to highlight world-class athletes in their categories.

In 2008, NOPT knows the greatest success in the face of Mougiou Dimitri, who along with Vassilis Polymeros won the silver medal at the Beijing Olympics, just before they were already world champions in the double skiff rowing lightweight men.

Apart from the rowing NOPT displays a strong presence in the sport of canoe-kayak. Becoming three times first in the overall ranking of medals, Champion Club National Championship in the 2000 National Championship and Development in 2004 and 2006.

The oldest sport, skiinghas got life from the foundation of NOPT the 1971 and trainig is deing done in facilities in Drepani location and the Trizina Neorio Poros.

The department is supervised by Sotiris Cypriot pan-European Slalom Senior 1 Champion for several years Champion. Today it has about 10 active athletes with high distinctions World and European level as well as many gold medals nationwide.To supplement the water workouts, NOPT has got Training Ground for its athletes.

## Beaches

Poros, despite its small expanse, has many beaches, almost all of them along the southern and overgrown coastline of the island.

Most beaches are close to the town of Poros and one can get there by car, bus, bicycle, or by foot, but also by small boats from the port.

After the small bridge, on the left and west, the coastal road passes Perlia and meets successively the Mikro Neorio, the Megalo Neorio, the love's bay and the Russian naval bay, very beautiful beaches where the pine trees reach the sea.

On the right of the small bridge there is the most close beach of the town of Poros. It is a sandy and organised beach with the name Kanali.

After the small bridge, on the right, the coastal road continues towards the east and meets first Askeli and then Monastiri, two picturesque and clean beaches with amazing view.

After Askeli and before the Hotel Sirene Blue Resort, the coastal road goes to the Temple of Poseidon. After the Temple the road descends and lead us to a close picturesque cove where the Vagionia beach is.

Also there are beaches opposite Poros island, in Galata. You will find there the sandy beaches of Plaka and Aliki, which are worth your visit.

## Perlia
After the canal bridge is located Soinikismos that first inhadited from refugees from M. Asia. Left, towards west, is the location Perlia, a beautiful location with picturesque tavernas and rooms/apartments to let.

It is located opposite Progimnastirio, very close to the town of Poros and is ideal for family tourism and relaxing vacations, only 10 minutes on foot from the port of Poros.

For your accomodation in Perlia there are the "Drossinos Studios", the "Matrona Apartments", the "Christina Perlia Studios" and the "Niki's Village", while for your food there is the picturesque tavern of "White cat", above the shore.

Perlia has got at its right the beach Mikro Neorio, a very beautiful and organised sandy beach, only 500 meters away; and at its left the beach Kanali, another organised sandy beach 150 meters away.

## Russian Bay

The Russian Bay a beautiful and picturesque bay, which is classified as a historical monument, because of its great architectural and historical interest.

On the opposite side is Daskalio, a small island with its lovely church. Then there is the Gerolimenas a secluded pebble beach, which is across the islet of Petra.

We have an organized beach with deck chairs, umbrellas, tables and a canteen where you can eat a snack, drink your coffee, cool down having an ice cream or soft drinks, ouzo, wine and beer.

Its 400 meters away from Neorio, where there are the Pavlou Hotel, the Agyra Hotel, the Kaikas rooms to let, the Maria Mourtzoukou rooms to let and the Studios "Simeon".

Also at Neorio there are the Restaurant "Vasilis", the Restaurant of the Hotel Pavlou and the Restaurant of Agyra Hotel. Vessels of all sizes, small and large, are moored in the gulf several times adding extra glamour to the area.

## Vagionia

Vagionia is a quiet organised beach with sand and pebbles situated in the northern part of the island, ideal for relaxing holidays and all kinds of fishing, especially snorkeling.

There, you can find beach chairs, umbrellas and a cafe snack bar, where you can grab a snack, drink your coffee, have an ice cream, soft drinks, ouzo, wine and beer.

The beach is located in the bay of Vagionia, facing the open sea and is opposite the island of Aegina and Piraeus.

A sunken city is found at the sea bottom where one can even distinguish the cobblestone roads and the foundations of ancient households.

Coming in from Poros, after passing the bridge, keep left heading for Sinikismo and follow the twisting road among large pine trees which leads you to the restaurant "Paradeisos". Shortly after the tavern you will come across a small sign where we make a left and go down to Vagionia.

## Mikro Neorio

After the canal bridge, on your left going westward, the coastal road leads you to Mikro Neorio, a beautiful sandy beach with umbrellas, deck chairs and a small canteen. The pine trees here stretch out to the sea. Mikro Neorio is one of the most beautiful beaches in Poros, where the pine trees reach the sea as well.

At the canteen you can eat a snack, drink your coffee, cool down having an ice cream or soft drinks, ouzo, wine and beer. Vessels of all sizes, small and large, are moored here.

Mikro Neoreio has continuous taxi or boat routes to the center of Poros. If you feel like walking, it takes about 25 minutes.

## Kanali

**Kanali** is located after the bridge that connects the Pregymnasium with Sinikismo and has the advantage of going there on foot.It's just 8 minutes away from the port of Poros with a divine sandy beach in the heart of the bay of Askeli.

At the sandy beach there is the cafe beach bar "Kanali" for coffee, drinks, beverages and ice creams. Also above the sea and with amazing open sea view there is the tavern "Kanali", where you will find a variety of mediterranean cuizine , meat on the grill and pies, to taste after your swim.

Kanali area has got Apartments/Rooms to let, the "Canali Beach Hotel", the "Kanali Apartments" and the "House of Irene".

You can also find a supermarket, mini market and a bicycle rental shop which are convenient for family travel.

Accompanied by a good book, you can indulge yourself by drinking a coffee or refreshment as you're relaxing on a sunbed under the beach umbrella with a table.

## Neorio

After the canal bridge, on your left going westward, the coastal road leads you to Mikro Neorio, a beautiful sandy beach with umbrellas and deck chairs. The pine trees here stretch out to the sea.

The road continues and reaches Megalo Neorio, one of the most beautiful beaches in Poros, where the pine trees reach the sea as well. Neorio is an ideal destination for a relaxing family vacation and is located opposite the Peloponnese, in the bay of Poros.

For your accommodation in Neorio you will find Hotels and Rooms/Apartments to let next to the beach. There are the Pavlou Hotel, the Agyra Hotel, the Kaikas rooms to let, the Maria Mourtzoukou rooms to let and the Studios "Simeon".

You can eat after your swim next to the sea, at the shore and enjoy traditional greek cuizine with barrel wine. There are the Restaurant "Vasilis", the Restaurant of the Hotel Pavlou and the Restaurant of Agyra Hotel. Delishious cooked meals, fresh fish and sea food from our local fishermen, meat on the grill and anything else.

You will find Pool Bar, Supermarket, water ski and games school. The beach is suitable for racquetball and the sea…. for all kinds of aqua sports.

Megalo Neorio is very close to two other very beautiful and picturesque beaches of Poros, the Love Bay and Russian Naval Base, located on the coastal road after Neorio.

## Askeli
After the Kanali, the coastal road continues and leads to Askeli, located a few kilometers northeast of the port. Askeli faces the open sea and is built amphitheatrically on the slope of a pine covered hill with a panoramic view from above.

There are four snake-shaped streets on the road starting from the beach road and branching out across Askeli, reaching the top of the hill.

It has an organized beache with a beach bar, beach volley, tables and chairs, deck chairs, umbrellas, showers, rooms to change, rest rooms and water ski training school. There is space to play racquetball and tall trees to rest underneath them.

Askeli has large beach hotels, with pools, bars and restaurants but rooms and apartments to let are also available. Beautiful homes perched on the hillside with excellent views and cool breezes for those who have their own means of transportation or are willing to walk.

Askeli is another perfect place for families as most homes have, among other things, apartments with a kitchen and everything else that a family may need.

It has a supermarket, minimarket and bicycle or scooter rentals for short excursions. There are also poolside cafes and snack bars where you can enjoy a swim. Severalcafe snack with delicious food, coffees, ice creams and reasonable prices are located here.

At the coastal road, in front of the sea there is the tavern "Olga's", the "Panorama", the "Askeli", the restaurant of the Hotel "New Aegli", the bistro "Odyssey's Corner" and the grill house "Colona-Askeli" with good food and reasonable prices

## Aliki & Lemon forest
Aliki is a very beautiful organised beach with sand. It ends in a small sea-lake. It has got shallow waters and in front you can see the islet of Bourtzi with the castle of Eidek, where someone can go by swimming.

Aliki is an organised beach with sun umbrellas, deck chairs, canoe and water bicycles. It has got pictursque tavernas above the sea and a modern hotel complex with restaurant and cafe snack bar next to the sea.

Aliki is located opposite of Poros island, next to the famous lemon-tree forest, a large area which used to have over 30.000 lemon trees and orange trees with tavernas and a lot of waters. From above the view is panoramin. It is the special place of Poros, where many famous poets and artists took inspiration from.

## Love's Bay

The Love's Bay is a very romantic cove where one can enjoy the green and turquoise water swimming ... under the lush pine trees!

Once again, we have an organized beach with deck chairs, umbrellas, tables and a canteen where you can eat a snack, drink your coffee, cool down having an ice cream or soft drinks, ouzo, wine and beer.

Its 200 meters away from Neorio, where there are the Pavlou Hotel, the Agyra Hotel, the Kaikas rooms to let, the Maria Mourtzoukou rooms to let and the Studios "Simeon".

Also at Neorio there are the Restaurant "Vasilis", the Restaurant of the Hotel Pavlou and the Restaurant of Agyra Hotel.

Vessels of all sizes, small and large, are moored in the gulf several times adding extra glamour to the area.

## Monastiri

The Monastiri is located on a hill in the east coast, at the coastal road after Askeli and Sirene Hotel. Right under it is a quiet and organised beach with crystal clear water, under the omonymous Monastery of Zoodochos Pigi, next to a pine forest.

The area offers water sports and snorkeling. Also available in the area are sunbeds, umbrellas and a canteen where you can have a snack, ice cream or drink your coffee, soft drinks, spirits, wine, ouzo and beer.

To the Monastery location, right above the sea you will find the hotel complex "Sirene Blue Resort", a few minutes from the Monastery. It is a very beautiful hotel, built at the slope of the hill, and reaches to the sea.


## Folklore

### Traditional customs
*What did they wear in Poros - Troizinia*
Despite the fact that Poros is an island, however, the insular suit had never been worn, but the "fustanella" had prevailed for men. The women wore rather costumes of continental country, despite islander.

After the arrival of Kapodistrias, even more people started wearing European costumes, in such a grade that around the 1860, those who were still wearing a "fustanella" were few, and in particular, the elders.

In this contributed the fact that Poros was near the capital, its residents had frequent communication with the capital's residents, and they were adapted easily in the new customs. In 1912 the costumes had been completely europeanised, and only a few insisted on a type of fustanella, mainly residents of the countryside.

In 1950, the women of Poros of the ruling class were competing in who would sew the fairest dress, mainly in Athens, in order to make an appearance in various dancing parties that were held in Poros, the most of the parties and the official ones, in the hall of the Progymnastirio

## Pistrofia

A few days before the feast of Saint Dimitris, and the latest until the first 10 days of November, herdsmen and other shepherds were starting from Valtetsi with their families and flocks to make the long and difficult travel for the winter in Poros and the opposite coast, where they had their huts and were spending the winter. Someone could see crowds leaving from Valtetsi forming a distant row, others on animals, and others pedestrians, others were carrying things and others were not. On their horses and mules, they had uploaded everything that would need, even long sticks that they had in order to set up their huts on the mountains.

On the front, the women were going with the leather swings that were called "nakes", hung on the shoulders, while other women were holding the newborn cossets in their arms that had still a difficulty in running. Behind them, the flocks with the young people and the children were following. Someone could see children, running and shouting at the herd dogs in order to collect the flocks. On the mules there were still cauldrons, churns and "levetia", hollow-ware, wash tubs, hens hung with their head down from the pack saddle, bundles with clothes and blankets and various other things that were needed. For almost 10 days someone would see the same setting. Herdsmen with their sheep pens were abandoning Valtetsi, until the village was getting empty. Back to Valtetsi almost none was staying.

Leaving from Valtetsi, on the first day they were arriving at Aegioritika and were spending the night near the village Steno. On the second evening, after they had passed Achladokampos, they were arriving and were spending the night on the mountain, over the Mills. On the third, they were arriving outside Anapli and were spending the night near the village Lion, while on the fourth evening they were arriving and were spending their evening near the village Iria and on the last fifth evening, they were spending it in Choriza, near Ortholithi. From there others were going to the area from Kokkinia until Galatas and others were going to Thermisi and the region of Hermione. A lot of families were passing to the island and were herding their flocks in the pasture lands of Poros.

The road of return to Valtetsi was beginning always on the next of Saint George's day. They were following almost the same way, the same passages and in five days time they were arriving in Valtetsi, where the snow had melted and the mountains of Arkadia had bloomed.

But as the years passed by, a lot of families, because they were tired of this journey, they gave all their economies and bought big extents, where they were passing their winter. These extents began from the kerbs of Hermione and reached up to Damala, current Troizina. Some of them purchased also extents in the island of Poros. Thus, all these people stayed permanently in Poros and in Galatas.

And this beautiful valtetsian tradition of "pistrofia" lasted until the decade the ' 60.

**Gum resin collectors of Poros**

The profession of the gum resin collector, like many other professions, has been abandoned. The gum resin collectors in Poros were many, as the island was full of pines. A big extent was exploited by the Monastery of Poros. The Abbot every three years was delivering the exploitation of pines, which was usually been taken by the tradesmen of gum resin, but also by manufacturers of treatment of resin, from Lavrion, Chalcis and Eleusis. Slowly in the decades of 1910 and 1920 resin collectors from Agkistri settled permanently in the island and many of them bought their own pinewoods.

The work of a resin collector was difficult, intense, hard and with low wages. The resin collector was leaving from his home before dawn in order to arrive at the place he worked before the first light of day.

The work of the resin collector was beginning in almost the mid of April and was finishing in the end of October. The resin collector was chopping the pine with the pecker, a pecker that was especially used for pines. The chop, "hit" as the resin collectors used to call it, was becoming at the down part of the trunk of the pine, making a vertical peeling that had width six to eight cm. The "hit" of the pine needed a lot of technique, since the skin should be come out very thin, like a paper, so that the pine wouldn't get hurt in depth.

On the base of cutting, he was stocking firmly a small, iron, triangular bowl, "gkrava", where the resin of the tree was pouring like a teardrop. The "Gkrava» could have room for almost half a kilo of resin. The next year, they were chopping the pine, beginning from the top of the old section and over it. The care of the resin collector was to take the resin from the pine, without however creating cuttings that would be mortal wounds for the tree.

They were transporting the resin to the factories of treatment of resin of Eleusis, Chalcis and Lavrion. From the process of the resin, colophony, pitch-black and tar were produced, which were used in the old days for the caulk and the graving of the sea boats. Also, they were putting resin into the must in order to become Retsina.

## Lumberjacks and coalmen in Poros and in Galatas

The coal (charcoals) during those years was made with the forge fires of coal. These were forge fires made of wood. The coalmen were making a team of three to four individuals that were between them relatives or friends. They were coming in agreement with the owners that had big extents and other land owners of the region and were taking the "topiatiko". The "topiatiko" was the land plot that the coalmen were taking and the rent they were paying to the owners. The most of the times they did not pay, as it was after the clearance of the ground that the extent was becoming a fertile field. Many of them were going to Kokkinia and to Mpelesi, in governmental extents and so they didn't have to pay the rent. Others were making forge fires on the island.

The coal forge fires were becoming mostly during the winter months and lasted from December until April, in years however that there was no olive oil production and the olive oil presses were closed. The cutting of the woods however could become all year long. Thus, after they were removing plenty of logs and were cutting a lot of timbers, they were choosing a flat surface, in a place with no wind and near water. The surface of space of the forge fire was circular, flat and they were opening a channel around it, so that the waters wouldn't enter in the space of the forge fire.

The construction of the forge fire was made with a practical way. They were measuring the area of the forge fire with the steps, Eastern to westwards and afterwards north to southerly. If the steps were 6 roughly metres, the forge fire would produce a thousand to a thousand and two hundred kilos of coal, while if it was 8 metres, the production of coal would approach the 2.000 kilos. The construction of the forge fire needed technique and one from the team, was the craftsman that was undertaking the building.

After they were finishing the building, they were covering the forge fire with branches of wild locust tree, lentisk or venia and over the branches they were covering the forge fire with dirt, the "karvounistra". Then, they were throwing from the "mpoy'ka" dry timber, firebrands and small dry logs and they were turning on a fire. They were leaving it to burn for almost 10 hours and afterwards they were covering the exit of "mpoy'kas" and were opening in distance of half metre from the top two holes from the both broadsides of the forge fire, so that the forge fire could take air and could keep the fire alive. When one day was passing by, they were closing these holes and were opening four holes half a metre lower than the first ones and so on they were reaching in the base where they were opening more holes in order to strengthen the light of the timbers. The duration of the forge fire was lasting for almost ten days regarding to its size. The coalmen were keeping with shifts the forge fire day and night, because many times it was opening a big hole by itself, the fire was getting out and the whole forge fire was in danger to become ash and not coal.

Nowadays, there is no one in Poros who makes the work of a coalman.

**The fishermen of Pounta**

Since the old times, the neighbourhood of the fishermen in Poros was Pounta. In even older times, in all the sea wall, from the Museum up to near the Cross, someone could see boats with nets, longliners, boats for the catching of octopuses and other boats for flare fishing with the lamp of acetylene on the crow, next to trawls, gri - gri and wind trawls resting on their double irons, tied up with mooring cables.

Gaites and trehantiria, sakoleves and paparovarkes, all the fishing boats, all the beach from Vaggelistra up to the Cross was one big boot-yard. There, the old people of Poros were fixing and graving their boats.

The fishermen, fighters of the sea, are still making their work with the gear and the art that they ' learned from ' their fathers and grandfathers. Nets, harpoon and trawl line. In the older times, the flare fishing also worked with shining on the coast, slow paddle, the head in the glass, the harpoon in the hand and the abstention from the trawl linego on the side. Sometimes, when no patrol car of the port authorities seemed from the bluff, they were striking a very small part of dynamite, to remove live deceit for the trawl lines.

## Music and Dance
### The dance of Chasapikos of Poros

The Chasapikos dance is coming from Minor Asia. It was originally a male dance and owes its name from the Chasapides or the Makelarides of Byzantio.

While it was a clearly traditional dance, after the great popularisation of bouzouki and baglamas, it began to be danced in different ports and in cities.

It was choreographed and was developed in something entirely different from its initial origin. Nowadays, it is danced by men and women and has been promote in such a range that is regarded, mostly by the foreigners, as the most representative Greek dance, also known as syrtaki.

In Poros, a different choreography prevails, known as "the Chasapikos of Poros". It is influenced by many places of Greece and is enriched with the phantasy of the "Meraklides" (people with talent, will and eagerness) of Poros.

The Chasapikos of Poros, since the beginning of the 50's, was danced by local inhabitants on boats, in taverns, celebrations and festivals also for reasons of living.

It is very impressive and manful dance and is regarded today as one of the most beautiful dances of chasapikos in Greece.

*The choreography of Poros is consisted, except of the classic steps of chasapikos also of the following figures:* Halfs | in/out | "surta spasta" | Pireaus | Sotiris | half closed | Koulouri | ntoulpes

*Other older figures are:* Stavreas | jumped or seated ntoulpes No 1 or No 2

The dancers are choosing what figures they want and with any row. The musical meter of Chasapikos is 2/4.

## Music - Bayianteras

One of the greatest pages of the history of the Greek music was written at the yards of Piraeus and at the islands of the Saronic, by Mitsos Gkogkos.

Dimitris Gkogkos was born in 1903 in Piraeus. He was the 22nd child of the non-commissioned officer of the Port Corps, Yannis Gkogkos.

Dimitris started learning music from a very young age, from 7 years old; he started playing the mandolin, then the guitar, the violin, the bouzouki and the small bouzouki. He was educated (certificate of an electrician).

Since 1925, when he made a new version of the Italian operetta "Bayantera" of Erich Kalman for a public orchestra, he took the nick name "Bayanteras". Just a while before the decade of 1930, he plays in the Piraeus' industrious pitches of the port.

He obtains a tight relationship with the protagonists of the rempetiko, Markos Vamvakaris, Stratos Pagioumtzis and the Methanian George Batis.

In 1937, he records his first disc and since then he composed unforgettable hits, like "Chatzikyriakeio", "A fish boat starts", "I was leaving alone without love", "My mind twinkles like it would be enchanted" etc. In 1941, Bayanteras lost his vision, while he was singing on the stage, by a fast evolvent glaucoma.

During the German Possession, he participates in the Resistance with his lyrics, his music and his rebellious heart, by composing rebellious songs.

He died in his home, in Saint Ierotheos, with only companion, his "lady" Despoina Arampatzoglou, smoke worker and lyricist, in 1985.

## Customs
### Christmas - New Year's Eve

Many of the following customs have their beginning before the Turkish possession.

In Christmas, besides the necessary pig sticking, the Christ breads, the cookies and the almond toffees, since the old years, the carols during the Christmas Eve- were the precursors of the celebration of Christmas.

At that time, they didn't decorate a "tree"- this came to Greece in 1850 by the Bavarians of Othonas- they decorated, though, every kind of floatable with lights. That's why today we decorate small ships on land. Since 1868 when the Cretans refugees had come to Poros, the "skaltsounia" were also added in the delicacies.

On the New Year's Day besides the carols, the St Vasileios pie with the coin, the "melomakarona" (candies with honey) and the sugared short-breads, necessary was the "first foot", which everybody wanted to be made by a little kid, who was naïve and pure. And the kid had to go with a pomegranate, which the kid was breaking, so that the house will be full like the pomegranate, or a rock, so that everybody would be strong like it. Of course, the homemakers were giving candies and money to the child.

During the old years, a big importance was given to the hunting of the goblins that for twelve days, as they believed (Christmas - the celebration of the Lights) were excruciating not only the humans but their animals too. That's why after the benediction of the waters, they were taking holly water and were sprinkling every edge of their buildings, the people and the animals also.

**Halloween**

Halloween was celebrated in Poros since the very old times and the disguised people were the main characteristic of each era. Since the Halloween feast started, people were dressing either like Africans, or like Eptanesians, or like islanders, or they were wearing colourful clothes and self-made masks, they were going out on the streets in groups but there had been never organized a carnival like the one of Hydra, which is dated since the era of 1700 (it revived in 1974). Since 1999, the Municipality of Methana organizes a carnival with a significant success.

This fact doesn't mean though that Halloween wasn't celebrated with cheer and dancing. But the celebration was more familial, a point of view that dominated due to the Arcadian influence.

Many People from Chios, Smyrne and minor Asia in general, "brought" the custom of the "bell people"- disguised people with bells- but they didn't draw the attention.

So, every kind of disguised people was a pleasant parenthesis but was not the reason for a mass celebration. Many Moraitans used to smudge themselves with smoke from the fireplace.

However, the inhabitants in Tsikno-Thursday were overcooking roast meat so that I would be smelled in the neighbourhood and were celebrating the "meaty" Halloween and then the "cheesy", when the young men were stealing macaroni and were putting it under their pillow to dream of with which girl were thy going to get married.

The Halloween of the decade of 1960 included except of many other customs that are still preserved, disguises of young boys and girls, who were 15 until 25 years old, in Pounta, in Saint George and Mprinia, where they were dressed like Apachides of Athens, gypsies, signori, etc.

They were also singing various Halloween songs, like the "smelly lemon", "listen to me to tell you about a great love", these days have it", "on a new boat I embarked", etc.

Many times they were making a "maypole". Those days, the youngest of the youth were also making the air balloons. A light garland, a pad of thin colourful paper and a cotton waste sprinkled with petrol or inside a can, which they were lighting up and were letting it to rise high. And they were competing who was going to construct the biggest one, and who was going to take it higher.

**The day of the Uptake**

On the Day of the Uptake, the inhabitants were going to the beaches for the "Hairy", a rock with seaweeds which the girls were putting under their bed, so that they would dream the men who were going to get married with. In parallel, they were catching sea urchins, limpets, crabs and other sea species. Also, they were collecting sea water and were sprinkling the house and singing in the same time:

"Outside the fleas and the bedbugs, inside the hairy experience".

Also, during the Day of the Uptake, they were collecting chamomile for the whole year and were putting out and were spreading out the entire trousseau on their balconies, so that they would be aerated

**Easter**

During Easter times, children were telling the carols on the eve of Lazarus, eating fish on Sunday and distributing branches from palm leaves and flowers at the church. About the traditions of Easter, the children were coming out to tell the Christmas carols on the morning of Good Friday, then the decoration of the Epitaph, the Procession, the red eggs, the Resurrection and the roasting spits.

From the old days the epitaphs of the four churches of St. George, St. Constantine, the Annunciation and Progymnastiriou meet in the main square in the Port singing 'The generations are all ...». Another tradition of Good Friday was the hanging and burning of Judas.

## Other customs ...

On the first day of May, the famous garland was created, on which the Minor Asians and mostly the Smyrneans, were also putting garlic so that the evil eye could be avoided. Many girls, of Arvanetian or Megaritian background, were giving on that day a garland to their fiancés, with flowers that had gathered from house to house.

On the 4th of June, was celebrated in Poros, with a big festival, the feast of the Mother Mary the Merciful in Plaka, a celebration that nowhere else is being held. From the Eve of this day, clarinets, violins, side drums, drones, dulcimers were making an extreme performance, while the pigs and the lambs that were roasted on the roasting jack, were having an amazing smell, which was reaching to a long distance. People were having fun with the folkloric songs; they were eating and drinking, while various street vendors were promoting their trade.

This custom lasted until the year of 1960, after then it started to fade. Nowadays, an effort is being made to revive this custom. Relative festivals were held in Saint Panteleimonas of the lemon tree forest, during the day of the Savior and on the day of the celebration of Mother Mary.

However, the festival of Plaka was more picturesque and interesting because it had uniqueness

The jump over the fire of Saint John is a custom that we see to be held every now and then these days by people of younger age. But during the old days, it concerned both young and older people. Because after the jump of fire, the girls were taking a vessel and were filling it up with from three faucets with the "still water". There calling it like this because from the moment they started until the time they would turn back, they shouldn't speak to anyone.

After that, they were putting the "rizikaria" into the vessel, various objects with which they would see their destiny. They were covering it with a white cloth and on the day of Saint John, a first born young woman was taking the objects one by one out of the vessel and like Pythia did, she was telling the future of the interested woman. Many times, the attitude was satiric. So, that's how the phrase "all these I am hearing in Klidonas" survived. Nowadays, the Municipality of Poros organizes the event "the jump of fire".

On the day of the Cross, the villagers were taking to the church a part of the seeds that were going to sow during the first rains, so that the priest would bless them. Then, they were mixing them with other seeds that had had left on the icons and were the last ones of the previous harvest, and then with all the seeds that were going to sow (it was of no matter if they were wheat, barley, pulse etc).

The Peloponnesians had also transferred the custom of the roasting pan: on the day of the Cross, the children of the neighbourhood were taking a copper roasting pan, were going to the priest, he was giving a soul cake to them, they were cutting it in small pieces and the priest was sprinkling the pieces with "anama" (pure wine) and oil. Then, the children were going from house to house and they were sprinkling the seeds of each family with these pieces.

The Minor Asians brought also with them the custom of "rags". When they wished for someone to get well, they were hanging rags from their clothes on a tree near the temple. However, this custom wasn't kept in Poros, but it survives in other places until today.

The Peloponnesians, when wanting to beg Christ and the Saints to cure someone of their relatives, were hanging various clothes on the icons. After the clothes were blessed, they were putting them in auction and the benefits were given to the church.

The funeral customs haven't been changed much today relatively to what was happening during the old years. The only ones that haven't been kept are the putting down or the flipping of mirrors and photographs as well as the smash of the glass plate when the dead body exits the house.

## Wedding and its customs

Much before the year of the 1821 and until 1920, the girls of Poros were married with the man that their father was choosing. As far as the customs of the wedding is concerned, there were various:

Arvanetean, moraitean, and insular in some cases, depending on the place of origin. Although the moraitean prevailed.

The engagement was happening before the wedding and this was the time that the groom was going to the bride's house with gifts. Then and until the wedding, which was happening too soon though, the groom wasn't allowed to see the bride again. At that time, the weddings weren't happening during the Lent. And almost all the weddings were happening during the summertime. The marriage was happening always on Sunday. From the beginning of the wedding's week, the friends of the bride, who were unmarried and pure as it was supposed, were helping her to be prepared. To prepare her wedding dress that was slowly evolving, with songs, like: "Today shines the sky, today shines the day, today the eagle marries the pigeon". And many others.

On the previous days, or even on the same day, the "proikia" (clothing) of the bride were delivered to the "proikologous", after they had been exposed for three days to the bride's family house in order to be seen by her relatives. The "Proikologoi" that were receiving the "proikia", were delivering to the bride gifts from the groom. When they did not transport the "proikia" to the house of the groom, where the bride would stay, they were leaving them at the door and the assembled people were sprinkling them with rice and were singing "my well-destined Bride", etc.

The marriage (the crowning) was happening in the house of the bride, where the groom was going with his whole family, his friends, the people he invited, with the escort of an orchestra. If the house was near they were going in procession, on foot. If it was far, they were going by decorated horses that another one nice decorated horse was following, which was without a rider. This was intended for the bride in order to take her to the house of groom. On the front, running on a horse, the "sycharikiaris" (the man who announces the congratulation news) was going, with a scarf flag on a stick with cross, in order to announce that "they were coming".

After the crowning, a very big fest was held, and also the relative gunfires were hit. On the evening, the groom was taking the bride and they were leaving. However the feast was continuing for three days, whenever in the house of the groom, and whenever in the house of the bride. These were the so-called "epistrofia".

During that time, they weren't distributing bonbonnieres. If there were bonbons, these were on the disk. In any case, since those years, the free girls were taking bonbons from the disk in order to put them under their pillow. The relatives were giving meat, pies and other things for gifts. The narrowest relatives should be bringing an entire lamb. The groom and the bride were giving shoes to their parents and their parents-in-law for a gift.

Later when the fear that the groom may took the bride without marriage and left was absent, the marriages were also held in the house of the groom. And when after the tear of 1920 the marriages began to hold exclusively in the church, if the houses were near, the groom and the bride were going to the temple in procession on foot, with the orchestra playing. And after the wedding, they were firstly going at the house of the bride and then at the groom's house and had fun. An irrefrangible custom for many years, in Poros also, was the custom of the demonstration of the bloody sheet, or the underwear of the bride - which for this case was open between the legs - after the first night of the marriage.

This was proving her purity and she would never wash them. She was having them as a proof. Of course, they may not be exposed in common view, but the mother-in-law had the obligation or even better, the right to see them and to realise. And it was a big shame, if the bride was not pure. They were exposing her as a prostitute and were sending her away. And such cases did exist. But also the opposite did exist. They hided it, but they gave a bigger "proika" to the groom, the "panoproiki"

## Birth of a child

Graphic were the customs that were relative to the birth of a child (1800). The midwife was carrying the stool of birth the selli - and when she was reaching at the house, she was opening the doors, the windows, the drawers; she was unlocking everything so that the child would come out easily. And those who helped should say that they saw an oil man on the street and his oil was poured, so that the baby would slip easily. If the labour was difficult, they were calling for the spouse, who was striking three times the ridge of the mother-to-be with his shoe and he was saying: "I was the one that charged you; I am the one that I unload you". After the birth, they were wrapping the mother with cloth, from the breast to the kidneys, in order not to get swelled. For eight days she wasn't allowed to see the stars and when she was getting off the bed she was stepping on an iron. Also, they were wrapping the newborn, being careful not to wrap (!) any bad thing in, and were giving amulets to it.

## Information
### Flora - Fauna
**Vegetation - Flora**

In Poros, just like on the other islands of the Saronic, the condition is obviously better, as far as the natural environment is concerned, comparative to Attica. Almost the entire surface of the island, except the sections of the North- North-east side of it, is covered by pine trees.

On the north- north-east side of the island, there are olive groves and some farms with lemon trees and orange trees. In the area of Fousa, are still cultivated some vineyards, by which the great Fousaetian wine is produced. On the north of Fousa, on the mountains, bushes and brushwood are found, with the most dominant, the oak trees, the lentisks, the bretia and the bearberries, while in the peninsula of Bisti, the venies dominate.

Sfairia is triangular stone palisade that has three sides. The beds of stone are of trachyte and the vegetation is almost non-existing.

Nowadays, it has no natural source of water. Its coasts have totally 3.650 m. length and are extended towards three directions. It is volcanic and came from an explosion of the volcano, from which Methana also came, during the pre-historic years.

**Fauna**

The geologic bedrock (limestone), the physiognomy of the flora and the climatic conditions do not allow the existence at the area o f a big variety of species of land fauna and bird-fauna. The species that are noticed are rabbits, wild bunnies, badgers, mice, hedgehogs, turtles and ferrets. On the opposite Troizinia, there are also wolves, coyotes and foxes.

In the whole Troizinia, from the side of lizards, the tree snake (dragkolia), the asp, the arrow snake, and rarely the viper live there.

From the side of birds, there are many in the area, like the crow, the swallow, the swift, the sparrow, the owl, the gkionis, the gowk, the sea bird, the wild dove, the wagtail, the butcher bird, the kotsifi, the redneck, the karakaxa and various other singing birds, like the chaffinch, the goldfinch, the greenfinch.

Also, the emigrating birds that visit the island are the trugoni, the quail, the babbler, the woodcock, the apiarist bird and the fig eater.

The marine ecosystem of the era is healthier than the one of the North side of the Saronic and presents a pretty big variety of population and species.

Among these, the main species that have been found are: the alevin, the sardine, the atherine, the gauros, the butt fish, the boneto, the red mullet, the koutsomoura, the codfish, the mullet, the goby, the mackerel, the safridi, the kolios, the sparos, the brassie, the bass, the khan, the sargos, the scorpio fish, the lithrini, the barren fish, the rofos, the sfyrida, the synagrida, the lauraki, the tsipoura, the octopus, the cuttle-fish, the devil fish, the moray eel, the mougri, the garfish and many other different species of sea kinds.

Lately, it has also been developed in the area an organized fish-culture and nowadays, five units function already that breed the lauraki and the tsipoura with satisfactory odds.

## Geography-Climate

*Geography of Poros island*
The island of Poros is located at the South-West part of the Saronic Gulf, in a distance of 32 nautical miles from the port of Piraeus. It is divided from the coast of Troizinia with a narrow canal, the narrowest point of which has just 350-400 meters width. Kalavria along with Sfairia covers a surface of 31, 2 sq. km. and is alpine, like

133

the whole Troizinia, but its crests have softer curves and, except of the few cultivated areas, it's almost covered with pine trees. The shape of Kalavria is triangular and from the main body of the island, three peninsulas are standing out. To the north, there is the peninsula of Bisti, which ends up to the cape of "Achedo" (Bisti), to the south-east the peninsula of the Momnastery is extended, which ends up to the cape of "Kalavri" (Modi) and to the north-west the peninsula of Neorio is extended, which ends up to the cape of "Ntana" (Fanari), which is named like this because on its end, a lighthouse is built, which shows to the ships the entrance of the Gulf of Poros.

The island of Poros consists essentially of two islands that are united with a small isthmus of 150 m. width, Kalavria, which is all over green, full of pine forests, olive trees and lemon trees, and Sfairia, which is rocky, arid, but very beautiful and picturesque. There, the city of Poros is built in an amphitheatrically way, while the District, Askeli, Neorio, Fousa are found in Kalavria and Aluki, Artemis in Troizina. In antiquity, Kalavria and Sfairia were parted with a part of sea, which was pretty deep, and they comprised two separate islands. For this reason, Sfairia didn't belong to the Kalavrian people, but to the Troizinians because it was closer to them. Pausanias, who visited the area on the 2nd century AC, reports that there was sea between the islands.

But the torrent that descends from the small vessel and the mountain of the Prophet Helias, transferring rubbles, soil, loose stones and sand, filled the sea that was between the two islands, united the two islands and transformed the channel that divided them into an isthmus that unites them. So, the place was created, where the district "Sunoikismos" is built nowadays.

This can be found out by the fact that the soil of "Suloikismos" is consisting of dirt and loose stones, which is of the same synthesis with these of Kalavria"s and are totally different from the bedrocks of Sfairia. The bedrocks of Sfairia are of trachyte, while the Kalavria's are of limestone.

In 1877, A small channel was opened in the isthmus, a small canal, of 125 meters length, 4,80 m. width and 1-2 m. depth. From this canal, the boats can pass from the cove of the Progymnastirio, which is towards Askeli to the port of Poros or Neorio.

For the communication of the two parts of the island, a small bridge has been constructed, which has width as the existing road, the known bridge of the Progymnastirio.

Nowadays, the whole island, Kalauria and Sfairia, is called Poros. This name was taken by the narrow sea that is found between the city of Poros and the opposite coastal beach of Galatas, which is also the pass (poros) of the ships from the port of Poros to Hydra or the opposite. This narrow sea to the side of Peloponnese has very low depth and the pass of the ships is passed only in a curvy way towards the coast of Poros from the place "Kolona", where the passengers' ships come along side until the exit of the pass, at the place "Cross".

The whole area of Troizinia belongs to the Nomarchy of Piraeus. The island of Poros (Sfairia Kalavria) has a population of 3.929 inhabitants (census of 1981). Troizinia includes coastal sections of the south-east Argolida, the peninsula of Methana and the island of Poros. It covers a surface of 291 square kilometers and has a population of 11.809 inhabitants (census 1981). To the Municipality of Poros also beling the districts Aluki, Artemis, Lemon tree forest, Monastery of the Life Source, Blue Coast and Saint Nektarios (Fousa).

## Morphology of the ground

In the centre of the island of Kalavria, two mountains prevail, which are overgrown with pine trees. On the east part, there is "Vigla" with 378 m. height and in the middle of the island, the"Prophet

Helias" with 314 m. height that on its peak, the homonym chapel of Saint Helias is built. The two mountains are uniting wit a neck of 1600 m. length, which is expanded at its beginning to the side of the Prophet Helias and a small plateau of 50.000 sq. m. is formed. It is "Polychron".

To the side of Vigla, this neck ends up to two small hillocks. On the hillock that is to the south, a small settlement is built, with approximately fifteen houses, and is named "Samuel". In an approximately 600 m. distance from "Samuel" and 1000 m. from "Prophet Helias", on the brow of the neck, the place "Palaces" is found, where there exists today everything has been left from the once upon a time bright temple of the God of the Sea , Poseidon. This place and everything standing in a ray of 500 meters around the sanctum of the temple have been abalienated and now belong to the Greek State.

The two mountains, "Vigla" and "Prophet Helias" are divided by a deep flume, "Tsoumpa", which beginning from "Samuel", reaches to "Askeli" and ends up to the place "Panagitsa". In some points of the flume of "Tsoumpa" waters gush that flow and got lost in the flume, even during the summer. In winter, when it rains, this dry river carries much water and is transformed into a torrent, which ends up to "Askeli".

The mountain "Vigla" on the north, descending to the sea, is divided into two hills. The west one is planted with pines and is smoother and reaches to the cove of Vayiona. On the north side of the hill, there are farms with olive trees and lemon trees. A bit down from the Temple of Poseidon and in a distance of 700 meters, the chapel of Saint Paraskeui is built.

The east hill is rocky, with bushy vegetation, ends up to the steep coasts of "Skarpeza" (Long channel). On the south-east of "Vigla", three pine-planted hills are formed. They are "Staurorachi", "Kokoreli" and "Tsoutsoura", the plains of which end up steeply to the cave of "Modi".

On the south of "Vigla", two calm hills are formed, which also are full of pine trees. They are "Kiafa" and "Kontita". On the plain of these hills, the great Monastery of the Source of Life is built, to which the biggest part of the around area also belongs.

The mountain of "Prophet Helias", which is found in the centre of the island, has on its north-west part, slightly smooth plains, also full of punes, there are also though many fields cultivated with olive trees that reach to the field of "Fousa". This field covers a surface of 300.000 sq. m., the biggest part of which is covered with vineyards that produce the great fousaetan wine. On the north-west point of

Fousa, the chapel of Saint Antony is built and some cottages are found around it.

On the east point of Fousa, the chapel of Saint John is built, while a bit further on the plain, the chapel of Saint Nektarios is built. From that place the calm hills start, full of olive trees and lemon trees that reach to the cove of "Vayiona". This is the place of "Kantali". At this area, many natural springs with flowing water exist.

**Climate**

The climate of Poros has a cool summer followed by a mild winder and there's constant breeze blowing from the North which ensures a clear horizon.

## Transport
*How to come to Poros island*
A. WITH "FLYING DOLPHIN" OR "FLYING CAT" FROM THE COMPANY "HELLENIC SEAWAYS"

From the port of Pireus there are daily departures of flying dolphins and flying cats for Poros, which take only passengers and no vehicles. The trip lasts approximately 1 hour for the flying dolphins and approximately 1 hour and 20 minutes for the flying cats.

For more information on the ship's departures from the port of Poros or to get tickets, you can call the travel agency Marinos Tours: (+30) 22980 - 23423, 22977, 22297 in Poros island.

B. WITH THE "AEGEAN FLYING DOLPHINS"

From the port of Pireus there are daily departures of Aegean flying dolphins for Poros, which take only passengers and no vehicles.

The flying dolphin makes the shedule "Piraeus - Aegina island - Agistri island - Methana - Poros island". The trip duration is approximately 1 hour and 45 minutes.

For more information on the ship's departures from the port of Poros or to get tickets, you can call the travel agency Askeli Travel (+30) 22980 - 29309 in Poros island.

The timetables are executed by Aegean Flying Dolphins : (+30) 210-41.21.654, 42.21.766

HOW TO COME FROM THE PORT OF PIRAEUS WITH FERRY BOAT

From the port of Pireus there are daily departures of Ferry boats for Poros, which not only take passengers but vehicles as well. The trip lasts approximately 2 hours and 30 minutes.

The first stop the ferry makes is at the port of Aegina, then it heads off to Methana and reaches its final destination which is Poros.

The timetables are executed by Saronic ferries: (+30) 210 - 4117341 / 4171190.

For more information on the ship's departures from the port of Poros or to get tickets, you can call the travel agency FAMILY TOURS: (+30) 22980 23743, 22549, 26329.

HOW TO COME FROM ATHENS WITH YOUR CAR

If you own or rent a car, you can easily get from Athens to Poros in appoximately 2 hours. Through Attiki Odos, get on the National Road Athens Corinth and make a left after the canal heading towards Epidauros (Corinth Exit 10 - Epidavros).

Drive for about 30 minutes and you reach the intersection of Epidaurus. Before getting there, you will see signs to Poros or Spetses. At the junction turn right and immediately drive under the bridge and make a left.

Then, follow the new road, making sure you don't miss the sign to Poros. At this point, slightly turn left for Poros and you will reach Galata in 25 minutes, via the coastal road, from where you can hop on a small ferry to Poros.

The road is an extension of the highway, good enough for the entire journey, with an average speed, it takes about 2 hours to get there.

The small ferries from Galata departures run every 30 minutes. There is a big public parking, which is free, where you can leave your car in case you want to go across Poros by boat in 5 minutes.

HOW TO COME FROM ATHENS WITH THE BUS

Athens - Galatas
There is a daily departure of a bus from the Peloponnese Station ( +30 210-5124910 - 11-12) at 16.30 which arrives in Galata, opposite the island of Poros, in about 2.5 hours.

# Spetses

## Spetses Today
Spetses, the lady of the Gulf Islands. It is the island of Matrozou and Boumpoulinas, and helds fairly the privilege of the National affirmation for their invaluable and decisive offer, during the Greek Revolution of 1821.

Here, the history meets nature and tradition. The amazing combination of pine and sea, creates spectacular views of natural beauty. Lacy beaches with golden sand, pebbles and crystal sparkling sapphire waters, give you moments of peace and serenity.

At the same time, it maintains features that remain unchanged over time.

The mansions of the captains of the last century with the local architecture, the picturesque Byzantine churches, he historic museums, the streets with the famous spetsiotic cobblestones, the picturesque shipyards and carriages are traditional elements that manage to fascinate the visitors for many decades and beyond.

In Dapia, the current port, there were cannons that defended the town. Today around the harbor there is the commercial center of Spetses.

Spetses have about five thousand inhabitants, which multiply every weekend and summers due to the easy access from either Kosta or from Piraeus.

There are so many the lures of the island, that it is the preference of Greek and foreign visitors for their vacations.

Spetses is an island with strong cosmopolitan nightlife and all around is beautiful, clean, tidy, the residents are welcoming, so Spetses constitute today one of the most popular destinations in our country.

## Touring Spetses Town
*From the port of "Dapia" to the "Lighthouse"*

The walk along the coast toward the NE end of the town shows many beauties. Starting from "Dapia" which means "reinforced spot" - with many cannons still decorating its walls - we meet first the noisy beach of St. Mammas, terminal of the buses towards other spots of the island, and also the meeting point for coffee, lunch or dinner.

Immediately after and up to St. Nicholas church we find te beach of St. Nicholas and the famous mansions, built in the 19th and 18th centuries. These houses are a sample of the cultural and economical growth of the island at a time.

Well known artists, as Nikos Maraslis who restores the painted ceilings of these residencies, work for the up keep of these houses and other traditional buildings on the island.

The cathedral church of St. Nicholas, the Metropolis, a part of the church building itself, bears in its courtyard the monument of the Heroes, sculpted by Byron Kesses.

St. Nicholas is one of the oldest churches in Spetses of post Byzantine cross style with the extremely finely crafted bell towel where the flag of the Revolution was hoisted in 1821.

Further along we come to the far end of the "Baltiza"(Old Port) passing by the traditional shipyards which are kept up to now transmitting from generation the secrets of the art of caulking the boats. We admire beautiful building - old and new - that keep up the island colour and the architectural tradition.

A most enchanting example is the modern settlement that was built in harmony with the environment called "Pityoussa" with its beautiful square and its popular "ouzene"

"Baltiza" apart from its natural and environmental attractions is also the mooring place for the private yachts as well as commercial ones. Furthermore it is undoubtedly one of the most famous spots for night entertainment.

At the end of the walk is the Lighthouse where one finds the "Panagia Armata" church. The church was built in order to honor the "Virgin Mary" who helped the Greeks to fight against the Turks on her birthday on the 8th of September 1822.

Inside the church we can admire the beautiful painting of the Battle made by I. Koutsis in 1887. Outside the church are two tombstones celebrating the memory of I.G. Koutsis, the captain and the historian Anargyros Hatzianargyros.

At the feet of the lighthouse is the garden of the canon battery - where we find the Hatzigianni Mexis canon batteries restored and the park where are scattered modern sculptures of Natalia Mela - a place of historical memory and relaxation. At the far end we see the bronze effigy of Kosmas Barbatsis, sculpted by Natalia Mela, offered to the town of Spetses and its people by one of the island's lovers, the French Annette Schlumberger.

*From the port of "Dapia" to the "Schools"*

Taking the seaside direction towards the NW of the island, the visitor will find it most interesting. Starting by the picturesque and noisy coffee shops as well as the "ouzenes"[ouzo bars] of Dapia, we choose for a while the interior road, in order to admire the beautiful architecture of the mansion, at present under restoration, of the benefactor of Spetse, Sotiris Anargyros.

This magnificent building - a jewel for the island with its neoclassical style and the two Egyptian sphinxes dominating the right and the left side of the entrance-, has hosted during its long life. The Town Hall, the Rothschild family and has also been the Cultural Center of the island.

Next to the Anargyros mansion is the "Pefkakia" square with its small forest and the house - museum of Bouboulina, overlooking the place. This lordly mansion with its unique carved ceiling in the big living room, functions as a museum with live guided tours where the visitor can hear about the life and work of Bouboulina and admire her possessions.

We continue our course by the sea road arriving first at the Bouboulina square where all importand fesivities take place, the best known of which is the re-enactment of the battle of Spetses of 1822, better known as "Armata". The imposing statue of Laskarina Bouboulina standing in the middle of the square is the work of the sculptor Natalia Mela.

The historical hotel "Poseidonion" borders the inside part of the square. Sotiris Anargyros had it built at the beginning of this century and since then the hotel has been visited by thousands of well known politicians, businessmen and artists. Its fine architecture and its nicely decorated interior attract till today the admiration of a different architectural view.

Some hundreds of meters ahead we find the old "Daskalaki" cotton mill factory, transformed today into a luxurious tourist compound, keeping and combining at the same time traditional and modern architecture. Further down stands the Town Hall, a traditional building decorated with beautiful pebble designs and a garden.

At the far end of this itinerary we come to Kounoupitsa where we admire the most renowned "Anargyrios-Korgialenios" school, that provided famous scientists, politicians and artists like I. Xenakis, G. Rallis and others, for over fifty years.

These unique installations that have been used for the last ten years are revived by the opening of a special Environmental Center under the supervision of the Ministry of Education, the Directing Committee of the Fountations and the Municipality of Spetses.

*From the port of "Dapia" to "Analipsis"*

Starting from "Dapia", we first cross the "Clock square", the most renowned square in the center of town, surrounded by all kinds of restaurants and bars. In its NW side stands the Town Clock built at the beginning of the century by George I. Leonidas.

We take the interior road, parallel to the seaside one towards the seaside one towards the Northeast, following the signs "The Spetses Museum" and we arrive at the Hatzigianni Mexis mansion where the museum is housed. Inside this important building, decorated with high arcades and the hero's head sculpted by Byron Kesses, the visitor will see archaeological findings and historical heirlooms of the Greek Revolution.

Continuing our walk we arrive at the triange of St.Eleftherios Church where the road separates in two directions.

To the Southeast [towards the mountain] it takes you to "Kokkinaria" and ends at the Monastery of All Saints and highter up at that of the Panagia the Gorgoepikoos.

The direction to the East comes to "Analipsis" square, where Easter is very traditionally celebrated. From there one road goes to the "Old Port" with its beautiful captain houses, and the other takes you to the Agia Marina beach and the regional road around the island.

*From the port of "Dapia" to "Kasteli"*

In order to go to "Kasteli" we leave "Dapia" taking the only road that starts where the horse buggies are packed and lead to the south direction of the island over the mountain.

At the height of the "Lazaros" taverna the road separates. To the right it climbs up to "Kasteli"[the island's fort], the region where the first medieval settlement was formed.

Walls surrounded the settling and its acropolis was situated where the church of St.Basil is now. At this very place was build the first town os Spetses as well.

Today the visitor can admire this pictursque neighborhood of Spetses with its church of St.Trinity, decorated with a fantastic wooden temple, the church of the Virgin Mary and that of the

Archangels. A natural fortification remaining as such up to our days is the torrent of St.George towards the East and that of Kounoupitsa to the West.

## The Island's Architecture

The houses in Spetses, either mansions or simple houses, has been built with a distinctive local architecture, combination of many elements.

The Spetsiot mansions, are witnesses to the cultural and economic development, which the island has seen in the late 18th century and continues until today.

The Manors are of two or three floors, with a garden and cisterns and the very rich were U-shaped, with a central building and two wings, right and left, as the home of Xatzigianni-Mexi.

The least wealthy houses are L-shaped, ie a main building and an annexe while somewhat rich ones had only one main building.

Other houses were yellowish and other white with many large windows and traditional tiled roofs, decorated with antefixes or small stone statues.
Many of the homes are from outside the leafs and inside shutters, and all open inward.

The more affluent homes had garden in the courtyard and cistern filled with rainwater. Almost all these houses had their yards decorated with mosaics from pebbles in different designs.

Downstairs is the kitchen which has a mouth pit communicating with the cistern, while in the first floor we have the bedrooms and the living rooms.

In the poor two-floor houses at the underground basement was the kitchen and the bedroom and sometimes laboratory or shop.

Most houses are surrounded by high fences, with characteristic large traditional wooden doors.

## The Island's Architecture

The houses in Spetses, either mansions or simple houses, has been built with a distinctive local architecture, combination of many elements.

The Spetsiot mansions, are witnesses to the cultural and economic development, which the island has seen in the late 18th century and continues until today.

The Manors are of two or three floors, with a garden and cisterns and the very rich were U-shaped, with a central building and two wings, right and left, as the home of Xatzigianni-Mexi.

151

The least wealthy houses are L-shaped, ie a main building and an annexe while somewhat rich ones had only one main building.

Other houses were yellowish and other white with many large windows and traditional tiled roofs, decorated with antefixes or small stone statues.

Many of the homes are from outside the leafs and inside shutters, and all open inward.

The more affluent homes had garden in the courtyard and cistern filled with rainwater. Almost all these houses had their yards decorated with mosaics from pebbles in different designs.

Downstairs is the kitchen which has a mouth pit communicating with the cistern, while in the first floor we have the bedrooms and the living rooms.

In the poor two-floor houses at the underground basement was the kitchen and the bedroom and sometimes laboratory or shop.

Most houses are surrounded by high fences, with characteristic large traditional wooden doors.

## The sightseeings

The historical square of Dapia: at the harbor, place of meeting of captains and rulers in 1821.

Today it is the center of tourism in the capital of the island with chairs and tables of the patisseries to have exploited even the last centimeter of space, next to the cannons used by Spetsiots fighters in the war of 1821.

The house of Xatzigianni Mexi:, first ruler and benefactor of Spetses. Here, at this house is the Museum of Spetses since 1939 that serves as archaeological and historical folklore collection, with relics of the Revolution, letters of Kolokotronis and Athanasios Diakos and the bones of Boumboulina.

Behind Dapia, the [Mansion of Boumboulina] with its unique carved ceiling in the great hall; was renovated and opened as a museum in 1992, with live tour during which the visitor hears about the life and work of Boumpoulina while seeing relics from the Revolution, personal belongings of the heroine and other interesting exhibits.

Also behind the port of Dapia, the exquisite neoclassical architectural stone Manor of the benefactor of Spetses S. Anargirou. This magnificent building on the island with the neoclassical style and the two Egyptian sphinxes dominate at the right and left of the entrance, stands out with the quality of its composition and structure. Today it is housing the Cultural center of Spetses.

**The Hotel "Poseidonio:"** vision of the benefactor of Spetses Sotirios Anargirou, contributed greatly to the development of Spetses. The «Poseidonio Grand Hotel» opened its doors for the first time in the summer of 1914, giving the island its cosmopolitan glamor. Located on the square Boumboulina, where all the big events on the island are being made, including the famous representation of the Battle of Spetses in 1822, known as "Armata".

The Anargyrios - Korgialenios School: nearby the hotel "Poseidonio", which was founded in 1927. Its excellent facilities spanning 130 acres with a private olive grove and additional 9,000 acres of private forest. The School comprises of 5 main buildings, of which 4 are designed and operated as a dormitory, while the main building area of 5,500 sq.m. has auditoriums (40-120 seats), conference and teaching room, press room, workshops, restaurant kitchen etc. It also has a classical outdoor theater for cultural events, a beach with water sports and sports facilities (football courts with nocturnal lighting, basketball , etc. ) .

The church of the Holy Trinity: built in 1793, the old metropolis of the island, build to the highest point of the city with magnificent carved iconostasis of the Assumption.

*Near the lighthouse, there is the church of Panagia Armata, built after the victory of Spetses, Hydra and Psara against the Turks, on 8 September 1822.*

The cave of Bekiris:, old haven of militants, in Agioi Anargyroi beach, behind the island, where the old Spetsiots hid the women in the Ottoman period.

The Old Port: with traditional shipyards kept up to date by transferring from generation to generation the secrets of caulk hulls. Along the waterfront restaurants, cafes, bars and clubs gives special glamor to night life and cosmopolitan style of Spetses.

## The Shipyards

Going towards the Old Port, just before it, we found the shipyards of Spetses, where tradition meets art.

Here our ancestors built the famous vrikogoletes, the boats that gave us our freedom, and Spetsiots continue the tradition of building vessels until today.

You can admire the beautiful vessels, others tied to piers and other under construction, from small fishing boats to luxury large boats of recreation.

Spetses, which has always been one of the largest shipbuilding centers of Greece, remains today one of the few places in our country which continues the tradition.

In the Old Port operate at least ten shipyards in which you can order from a small boat to a very large traditional wooden boat.

| | |
|---|---|
| Vaggelis Kobogiorgas | 22980-74055 |
| Giannis Boufis | 22980-73727 |
| Ilias Sklias | 22980-73743 |
| Panagiotis Theod. Belesis | 22980-72780 |
| Panagiotis Mix. Belesis | 22980-73150 |
| Vasilis Delimitris | 22980-72759 |
| Nikos Kalogiannis | 22980-73727 |
| Pantelis Korakis | 22980-72526 |
| Giannis Klisas | 22980-73107 |
| Nektarios Klisas | 22980-73935 |

# The History
## 1170BC and Earlier Evidence
The earliest evidence of man on Spetses comes in the shape of two Mesolithic flint spear-heads. These were discovered at Zogheria, and are thought to indicate a passing visit by hunters from the

Fraghthi cave on the mainland who were searching for water. Spetses' first inhabitants appear to have been mostly just passing through, on their way from the Peloponnese to the Cyclades.

We also know that around 1170BC, towards the end of the Mycenaean Era, the island was attacked by Mycenaean forces. It is considered a good possibility that ancient inhabitants of Spetses fought in the historic battle at Salamis, and that the island was attacked by Athenians during the Peloponnesian War.

Having passed through periods as a naval base for mainland cities, and as a part of the Roman Empire, along with the rest of Greece, Spetses was among the coastal areas left desolate by repeated pirate invasions. It is believed most likely that the majority of the islands inhabitants at this point in time sought refuge in the Roman-ensured safety of coastal towns on the Peloponnese.

## 15th to 18th Century
At the division of the Byzantine Empire, Spetses was given over to the rule of the Venetians, who were replaced by the Turks in 1460. Some time later came the Arvanite refugees from the Peloponnesus, who settled at first in the bays of Ag. Anargyri and Zogheria.

These new Spetsiots started out with just livestock, but quickly realized that there was a demand for the timber that came from the island's pines, and so began to build small ships to transport it. A second wave of refugees arrived in 1540, and the ships being built on the island grew in number and in size. After 1715, the small community which had established itself at Kastelli began to take shape as the mighty naval power which was to take part in the Orloff Insurrection in the second half of the 18th century. In retaliation for the Spetsiots' raising of the Russian flag, Turks and Albanians set fire to Kastelli in 1770, and many were killed or taken prisoner. When the first Russo-Turkish war ended in 1774, the prisoners were released and they returned to the island. The Spetses fleet now sailed under the safeguard of the Russian flag, and the island was in effect independent. It was governed by an 8-man council of elders, a local administrator and Turkish representatives appointed by the Spetsiot elders. This was a period of rapid economic expansion for the island, given further momentum by the outbreak of the Napoleonic Wars. The people of Spetses became extremely wealthy during this time, enough so as to allow them luxuries undreamed of in other parts of Greece, such as private tutors for their children.

## 19th Century
When the 1821 Revolution came, Spetses was the first of the Argo-Saronic islands to join the battle. The towns and villages of the Peloponnesus had already taken to arms, and the elders sent out a

call for support to their island neighbours. The reply came back without delay, despite the fact that due to their affluence, the Spetsiots did not suffer great hardships under Turkish rule. On April 3rd the Chancellery was taken without opposition, and the ships' captains swore allegiance to the revolution. The forces of Hydra were also enlisted, after consultations between the captains of both islands.

The Spetsiot fleet comprised of around 55 merchant vessels which had been converted into well-armed men-of-war. With names taken from Greek mythology, the magnificent armada liberated fortresses, blockaded ports and transported supplies. Their courageous crews also took part in the besieging and conquering of towns, which greatly speeded the arrival of freedom to the area.

The best-known of these brave warriors is also the only female admiral in Greek history, Laskarina Bouboulina. She was born in 1771 in a Constantinople prison to the Hydraean captain Stavros Pinotsis, who was at the time incarcerated there as punishment for his participation in the Orloff uprising, and would later die there. Her mother went on to marry the Spetsiot captain, Vassileos Lazarou or Orloff, and the family took up permanent residence in Spetses. At the age of 17, Laskarina married captain Dimitrios Giannouzas, who was killed in a naval battle with Algerian pirates.

Her second husband, Dimitrios Bouboulis was lost to her in the same way, and at the age of 30, Bouboulina found herself twice widowed with seven children of her own and four step-children from Bouboulis' first marriage to take care of.

Fortunately, financial worries were never a factor for Laskarina Bouboulina. She was heir to a vast fortune which she augmented by buying shares in a number of local ships and building three of her own, including the renowned "Agamemnon", which played a vital role in the revolution. Already a member of the "Friendly Society" (the organisation founded to cover the activities which would lead to the revolution), when the fighting began, she created and sustained her own unit of men, as well as crews for her battle-ships. She brought in weapons and supplies from abroad, which she concealed in secret hiding-places. All of this contributed to the diminishing of her once-great fortune, but enabled many important naval battles to take place. Her own personal sacrifices for the revolution were not limited to the financial burden, or even to her placing herself at the forefront of danger, as a much-respected Admiral of the fledgling Greek Navy. She also lost two of her beloved sons to the struggle for freedom from the Turks. After the Revolution had freed this part of Greece, Bouboulina lived in Nafplion with her daughter, until civil war erupted and claimed the lives of her son-in-law and his father. She then returned, embittered and close to poverty to her first husband's mansion in Kounoupitsa. It was here that this celebrated lady was to meet her inglorious end, murdered by a member of the Koutsis family in May 1825, when her son, Georgios eloped with their daughter.

## Into the 20th Century

After 1825, the Spetses merchant fleet continued to prosper for another twenty years, but then it fell into decline, taking with it the population of the island. The outlook for the island began to improve again with the return of Sotirios Anargyros from the U.S. in the early 20th century. Realising that the future for Spetses lie in tourism, he put his new-found wealth to the best possible use, constructing the road around the island, building the first hotel in the Greek islands (the Possidonion), and replacing the pine-forests of the island which had been depleted to facilitate the boat-building industry. Later he built the College which bears his name, and which for 60 years educated nobility from all over Greece.

During the German Occupation of Greece in the course of the Second World War, the Spetsiots suffered less than inhabitants of other places in Greece. Most people had a chicken or two, grew their own vegetables or fished, and so did not go hungry. There is, however, one notable incident which left its scar on the people of the island. A handful of Greek freedom-fighters were washed up on Spetses and hidden by the islanders in Bekiri's Cave at Anargyri. The German occupiers' informants leaked the news, and the people of Spetses were commanded to gather on the Dapia. There, the men of all ages were separated from the crowd and restrained. Aghast, the remaining islanders were told that unless they handed over the "andartes", the men's lives would be forfeit. The andartes were protected and helped off the island and the valiant men of Spetses gave their lives for the greater good.

The civil war which followed the release of Greece from the German occupation thankfully passed Spetses by to a great degree.

The island continued to produce various persons of note and standing, including Alexandros Diomidis, prime minister of Greece from 1950-1951. The 19th and 20th centuries also saw many noteworthy contributions from Spetses to the world of the arts, including poets Stratigis, Pergialitis, Logothetis, Botassi, and painters Eleni Altamoura, Ioannis Altamoura, I. Koutsis and D. Litsas.

## Geography

At 51 nautical miles from Piraeus, Spetses is the southern-most of the Saronic Islands. It has an area of 25.5km2, with its sole road, tracing the perimeter of the island, measuring 24km in length. The population of the island numbers around 4,000, the most of whom are to be found in the main settlement on the island, Spetses Town which spreads out over an area of around 4km along the coast. There are also a small number of summer houses and one or two hotels around the area of Ayios Anargyrios, on the opposite side of the island.

The first thing we see as the boat approaches Spetses is the white town with its red-tiled roofs, set against a back-drop of pine trees. Starting in the western corner, we can make out the 'Engineers' Settlement', elevated above the College, the Spetses Hotel, and the bay of Kounoupitsa, which is filled with boats and caiques. Coming in towards the town, there is the old Daskalaki Factory, now the Nisia Hotel, the imposing grandeur of the Possidonion Hotel (built in 1914, it's the oldest hotel on the Greek Islands), and the main harbour of the island, the Dapia, which literally translated means, the Fortress.

Spetses' architecture owes much to its sometime Venetian overlords, who brought with them Italian finesse, attention to detail and many Arab craftsmen who, in their turn, left their mark on the buildings of the island. Thanks to some (for once) sensible legal restraints, it is strictly forbidden to build modern and high-rise buildings. The beauty of the island today is also greatly indebted to the clause which the great benefactor, Sotirios Anargyros, added to his bequests to the islanders. Between 1913 and 1923, he had methodically bought up over 45% of the total island area, and this he left to the island of Spetses, with the prerequisite that the pine forest area ( he had re-planted around 100,000 trees during his lifetime), would never be built upon.

The fine old houses making up the town's interior can just about be seen from the sea. Above the Dapia and Possidonion rises the area of Kastelli, home to the first major settlement of the island. To the east, the tall bell-tower of St. Nicholas prevails amongst the old captains' houses, erasing, if it were really necessary, any doubt that you are anywhere other than Spetses.

The Old Harbour, or Palio Limani, is hidden behind the headland of the Faros (lighthouse) and glides into view shortly before the boat docks. Here the sun-seekers of the day who have metamorphosed into the fun-seekers of the night, will find most of the bars and clubs they have heard so much about. It is also the area that holds the most magnificent of the traditional-styled villas, many belonging to members of the European jet set.

Once disembarked, we are greeted by the freshly restored building which once housed the town hall of Spetses. The narrow inner streets, filled with shops as different and enticing as the wonderful mezes served with your lunchtime ouzo, provide a perfect place to stroll and while away the hours. The various roads out of town will take the unsuspecting traveller in different directions, which in their turn will reveal all the secrets that Spetses has hidden.

The highest point on the island is Profitis Ilias, at 285m. It lies roughly central to the breadth of the island and affords two spectacular views, to the north, of Kosta, Porto Heli and the Dydima mountains, and on the opposite side of the Argolicos Gulf, Leonidio, to the south. There are paths at various points on the island that will take you there, as well as to the many other Spetses beauty spots. These paths make for a number of lovely mini-hikes, all over the central part of the island.

Spetses has very little in the way of natural water supply, so the island's needs are met by the water-carrier boat which makes its daily trip from the mainland, and unloads at the Dapia.

The island was known, before the 18th century, as Pityousa, meaning "pine-clad". Then Albanian settlers corrupted the name to 'Petsa', which is what the island was called until the last century. The name Spetses, an Arvanite corruption of the Venetian 'Isola di Spezie' (Spezie: Italian word for spices), or 'Isle of Spices', more befits the island that we know today. The Venetians may have also called it 'Spezie' as it reminded them of the port on the west coast of Italy called 'La Spezia'. Due to two terrible fires in 1990, and 2000, the once dense pine forest is reduced to some, if still beautiful, much diminished untouched areas. Despite this, the island retains its natural beauty, not only in the remaining pines and the wide variety of wild flowers, but also in the vast array of aromatic herbaceous plants which grow beneath low-shrub thickets, pine and gorse. The most infamous of the herbs growing wild on Spetses is 'throubi', which is a kind of thyme with a particularly pungent smell. Local folklore has it that the smell of the throubi is responsible for the islanders being slightly crazy!

## Climate
### What to Expect from the Weather
Travellers to Spetses during the summer find it difficult to imagine extremes of weather when all they experience is the unrelenting heat of August! But Spetses does experience cold, wet winters and between 2000 - 2006 had a snow fall each year (these are normally very light - except in 2006 which was fairly heavy, high up in the hills). The information below is just a guide of the average weather to expect.

### Spring: April & May
The island has a short spring when temperatures range from 15 - 25 degrees Celsius. The weather is changeable still with the risk of sudden showers. Sea temperatures start to rise and many people,

especially those from colder climates, enjoy a swim in the sea. Spring is a particularly pretty time for the island with lots of flowers and greenery. The island is quite literally ablaze with colour. Evenings can still be a little chilly.

**Summer: June - August**
The weather on Spetses during high season is predictably hot, ranging from 25 - 38 degrees Celsius during the day. Humidity is low and rain fall during high season is rare but not unheard of. Sea temperatures increase to approximately 26 degrees by the end of the summer. August often brings windy weather that blows up from northern Africa so it's a warm/hot wind. Temperatures have been known to rise to 44 degrees during July and August.

**Autumn: September - October**
One of the most popular seasons on Spetses. The weather is still warm and while it's a little changeable, is still dependable enough to eat out in the evenings. Temperatures start to drop but the sea temperatures are high enough still to make bathing less bracing than it is in the spring. Nights become more bearable and it's a welcome change, after such a long hot summer, to put a light duvet or blanket on the bed.

**Winter: November - March**
The winter months are generally cold and damp with lots of rain. Most of the island is closed during these months. Temperatures

rarely drop below freezing. January - March are often punctuated with really sunny, warm days. These days aren't to be relied upon though, but viewed as a bonus. Very rarely there will be a sprinkling of snow on the very tops of the mountains, but as mentioned above, between 2000 - 2006 Spetses had a snow fall each year.

## Winds: Maistrali; Boukadoura; Pounentis; Bourini
Spetses is at the entrance to the Argolikos Gulf and because of this, the weather on Spetses is affected by the land-mass of the Peloponnesus. To the north, Argolida is 3km away, to the west at 30km lies Leonidio, while to the north-west, the bay extends 50km all the way to Nafplion. The various winds are all dependant on the difference in temperature which the sun creates between the sea and the land.

The weather is invariably good when there is a natural change-over in the winds, i.e in the morning, the maistrali (mistral), from the west, and in the afternoon, a boukadoura, or batis which comes in from the south or the east.

Maistrali
After sunset, temperatures drop on the Peloponnesus land-mass, and the cool air from it begins to blow towards the sea. It can begin in the first few hours of the new day, and usually begins to weaken

with the dawn, around 8am. It has normally completely gone by midday.

## Boukadoura (Bati)

In the meantime the sun has risen further; the mass of the Peloponnesus warms, and pulls on the air above the sea, so the wind blows from the south-east in towards the Argolikos Bay, with greater force in the afternoon. If there is no boukadoura in the afternoon, this is taken as a warning by the locals to expect intense west winds, or the pounentis.

## Pounentis

This is caused by cool air masses coming from the north-west straddling the sea, and trapping the evaporating damp air close to the sea's surface. This in turn causes a heavy mist and reduces greatly visibility close to the horizon. The barometer drops and the waters rise. After midday, there is no breeze at all, and it becomes very warm. With the sunset, when the land temperature drops, the cool air sweeps down to the sea with great force. This is when all hell breaks loose on the jetty of the Possidonion, as many boat owners are wont to carelessly go off for a relaxing meal, leaving their vessels to the mercy of the weather.

## Bourini

The bourinis appear at the end of August, beginning of September from the west, with tall, crashing waves, strong winds and heavy rain. Before a bourini, it is hot, hazy, and the barometer drops. The horizon towards Nafplion darkens with clouds, and the storm will usually break just before sunset.

All the above phenomena generally apply to the summer. During the winter there are south and north winds from other weather systems.

## Culture

### Archaelogical findings

Several excavations were conducted during the last century and they brought to light the follows:

Ceramics of the firsthellenic period or the 3rd millenium BC in Agia Marina. Protobyzantine, Paleochristian churches in Baltiza. A Byzantine settlement in Zogeria.

The bronzeage shipwreck of Dokos (2.200 BC), considered to be the oldest known in the world. The Mycenaean shipwreck of Iria (approx. 1200BC).

The procedure of cleaning and restoring the findings, a minute and difficult work that requires patience and time, takes place in specially arranged rooms of the Museum of Spetses, the safest and best organized museum in the region.

## Archaelogical findings

Several excavations were conducted during the last century and they brought to light the follows:

Ceramics of the firsthellenic period or the 3rd millenium BC in Agia Marina. Protobyzantine, Paleochristian churches in Baltiza. A Byzantine settlement in Zogeria.

The bronzeage shipwreck of Dokos (2.200 BC), considered to be the oldest known in the world. The Mycenaean shipwreck of Iria (approx. 1200BC).

The procedure of cleaning and restoring the findings, a minute and difficult work that requires patience and time, takes place in specially arranged rooms of the Museum of Spetses, the safest and best organized museum in the region.

## Historical Personalities
### Xatzigiannis Mexis

Hatzigiannis Mexis was born on Spetses in 1754 and was given the name "hadj"[hatzi] while visiting the Holy Lands. He acquired a considerable fortune and became famous.

In 1818 he received the title of "Nazir"(First among first) of Spetses by the Sultan, with the right to appoint and/or fire the beys.

He was the first to promote the revolution in Spetses, Hydra and Psara. His ships "Epameinondas", "Themistoklis", and "Periklis" has taken action against the Turkish fleet even before the revolution.

His heroism during the naval battle of Spetses, on September 8th, 1822 was acknowledged by the whole nation. He continued his political activity after the end of the Revolution, becoming State Conselor, Senator, Proxy and Chief of Spetses. He died in 1844.

In 1924 his house was declared a historical monument and today houses the Museum of Spetses.

### Kosmas Barbatsis
Kosmas Barbatsis was born in Spetses in 1792 and died in 1887.

Although he did not come from a wealthy family and hence did not provide the Revolution with ships and arms, his courage and patriotism gave him a special place in the history of the Nation.

He joined the navy very young and fought in many battles [Geronda, Karifea, Nafpaktos, Preveza, Patras].

His moment of triumph was the attack of the turkish flagship with his fireship during the naval battle of Spetses in 1822.

This risky action forced the turks to flee, and determined the outcome of the battle and further to that of the whole Revolution.

After the end of the war, Barbatsis grew old on the island, honoured by his fellow Spetsiots for his heroism.

## Laskarina Bouboulina

The figure that dominated the naval operations of the War of Independencs in 1821 was Laskarina Bouboulina.

Daughter of the Hydriot captain Stavrianos Pinotsis, she was born in the prison of Constantinople in 1771. Her name Bouboulina, derives from her second Spetsiot husband D. Bouboulis.

When Bouboulis was killed during a battle with Algerian pirate ships in 1811, Bouboulina took over his trading operations and the preparation for the revolution.

She became a member of the "Filiki Etaireia", the secret organization which was preparing the Greek revolution all over Europe, and had the "Agamemnon", her flagship, and three more war ships built at her own expenses.

Finally, she boarded the "Agamemnon" and personally took part in the sieges of Nafplion and Monemvasia by sea, as well as in the attack of Tripolis by land.

She took part in the battle of Argos and other battles of the Peloponese at the head of her own private army.

She spent all her fortune in providing food, arms and ammunition for her sailors and soldiers during the War of Independance. Her daughter Helen married Panos Th. Kolokotronis.

Laskarina Bouboulina was murdered in Spetses on May 22nd, 1825, during a family feud.

### Sotirios Anargyros
Sotirios Anargyros born on Spetses in 1849 and has been the greatest personality of Spetses of the last century. He had migrated to Istanbul, Romania, Egypt, France and finally in England, where he is involved with tobacco.

Finally, in 1883, Anargyros migrates to New York and works in the great tobacco company of Tompson, which in the end inherits from him.

At 1894 he returns for the first time in Spetses, leaves and then comes back the next year and marries his second cousin Eugenia I. Anargyrou.
Anargyros with his wife returns to America, and after three years, sells his businesses and makes a lot of money.

With his base on Spetses, he continues his commercial activity in Greece. In 1904 he ends the construction of a luxurious and neoclassical mansion near Ntapia and in 1907 he manufactures by his own expense the first aqueduct on the island.

later he buys a large area, which he reforests, creating the famous pine forest of Spetses and also he opens regional roads on the island.

Also he builts the famous hotel "Poseidonio" which gave great impetus to tourism and highlighted Spetses island as a resort of the upper social strata. Kings, princes, prime ministers and prominent personalities from around the world were every summer as Poseidonio as Spetses Guests. In 1928 Spetses become the permanent anchorage area for the English fleet, resulting in the hotel's clientele to also include the officers of the English navy, allowing even greater glory.

The largest offer of Anargirou which really raised the level of culture of the island is the creation in 1927 of "Anargyreios and Corgialenios School", which was one of the pioneers of the country colleges and operated until 1983 with Greek and foreign students.

At the same time, a significant contribution of Anargiros was the creation of the fund in favor of war invalids.

He died on December 18, 1928 in Spetses, leaving his entire fortune to the School.

## Things to Do in Spetses

Here's one real plus for visitors to Spetses: Cars are not allowed to circulate freely in Spetses town. This would make for admirable tranquillity if motorcycles were not increasingly endemic. Now, a closer look at the island.

Despite a series of dreadful forest fires, Spetses's pine groves still make this the greenest of the Saronic Gulf islands. Even in antiquity, this island was called Pityoussa (Pine-Tree Island). Over the centuries, many of Spetses's pine trees became the masts and hulls of the island's successive fleets of fishing, commercial, and military vessels. In time, Spetses was almost as deforested as its rocky neighbor Hydra is to this day.

In the early 20th century, local philanthropist Sotiris Anargyros bought up more than half the island and replanted barren slopes with pine trees. Anargyros also built himself one of the island's most ostentatious mansions, flanked by palm trees, which you can see off Spetses's main harbor, the Dapia. Amargyros also built the harborfront Hotel Poseidon to jump-start upper-class tourism. Then he built Anargyros College (modeled on England's famous Eton College) to give the island a first-class prep school; John Knowles taught here in the early 1950s and set his cult novel *The Magus* on Spetses.

Today, Spetses's pine groves and architecture are its greatest treasures: The island has an unusual number of handsome *archontika* built in the 19th and 20th centuries by wealthy residents, many of them shipping magnates, some now owned by their descendants or by well-heeled Athenians. Many Spetses homes have lush gardens and pebble mosaic courtyards; if you're lucky, you'll catch a glimpse of some when garden gates are ajar. Like Andros, another island beloved of wealthy Athenians, Spetses communicates a sense that there's a world of privilege that exists undisturbed by the rough and tumble of tourism, which let's not mince words means you and me.

Spetses Town (aka Kastelli) meanders along the harbor and inland in a lazy fashion, with most of its neoclassical mansions partly hidden from envious eyes by high walls and greenery. Much of the town's street life takes place on the main square, the Dapia, the name also given to the harbor where the ferries and hydrofoils arrive. The handsome black-and-white pebble mosaic on Dapia commemorates the moment during the War of Independence when the first flag, with the motto "Freedom or Death," was raised. Spetses played an important part in the fight for freedom, routing the Turks in the Straits of Spetses on September 8, 1822.

Fortunately for attentive visitors, a number of Spetses's dignified villas have been converted into appealing small hotels, mostly based at Ayia Marina.

## Things to See in Spetses

Spetses town (aka Kastelli) meanders along the harbor and inland in a lazy fashion, with most of its neoclassical mansions partly hidden from envious eyes by high walls and greenery. Much of the town's street life takes place on the main square, the Dapia, the name also given to the harbor where the ferries and hydrofoils now arrive. The massive bulk of the 19th-century Poseidon Hotel dominates the west end of the harbor. The Old Harbor, Baltiza, largely silted up, lies just east of town, before the popular swimming spots at Ayia Marina.

If you sit at a cafe on the Dapia, you'll eventually see pretty much everyone in town who wants to be seen passing by. The handsome black-and-white pebble mosaic commemorates the moment during the War of Independence when the first flag, with the motto "Freedom or Death," was raised. Thanks to its large fleet, Spetses played an important part in the War of Independence, routing the Turks in the Straits of Spetses on September 8, 1822. The victory is commemorated every year on the weekend closest to September 8, with celebrations, church services, and the burning of a ship that symbolizes the defeated Turkish fleet.

As you stroll along the waterfront, you'll notice the monumental bronze statue of a woman, her left arm shielding her eyes as she looks out to sea. The statue honors one of the greatest heroes of the War of Independence, Laskarina Bouboulina, the daughter of a naval captain from Hydra. Bouboulina financed the warship *Agamemnon,* oversaw its construction, served as its captain, and was responsible for several naval victories. She was said to be able to drink any man under the table, and strait-laced citizens sniped that she was so ugly, the only way she could keep a lover was with a gun. She was shot in a family feud years after retiring from sea.

You can see where Bouboulina lived when she was ashore by visiting Laskarina Bouboulina House (tel. 22980/72-077), in Pefkakia, just off the port. It keeps flexible hours (posted on the house), but is usually open mornings and afternoons from Easter until October. An English-speaking guide often gives a half-hour tour. Admission is 5€. If the Spetses Mexis Museum (tel. 22980/72-994), in the stone Mexis mansion (signposted on the waterfront), has reopened by the time you visit, you can see Bouboulina's bones, along with archaeological finds and mementos of the War of Independence. In the nearby boatyards you can often see caiques being made with tools little different from those used when Bouboulina's mighty *Agamemnon* was built here.

Check when you arrive for the new hours and fee. If you head east away from the Dapia, you'll come to the Paleo Limani (aka the Baltiza, or Old Harbor), where many yacht owners moor their boats and live nearby in villas hidden behind high walls. The Cathedral of Ayios Nikolaos (St. Nicholas) was built in the 17th century as the church of a monastery, now no longer functioning. The great moment here took place on April 3, 1821, when the flag of Spetses first flew from St. Nicolas's campanile as support for the War of Independence against the Turks. A bronze flag beside the church's war memorial commemorates this moment and a pebble mosaic commemorates the War of Independence (look for the figure of Bouboulina). While you're at the Old Harbor, have a look at the boatyards, where you can often see caiques being made with tools little different from those used when Bouboulina's mighty *Agamemnon* was built here.

## Best Restaurants in Spetses

Spetses's restaurants can be packed with Athenians on weekend evenings, so you may want to eat unfashionably early (about 9pm) to avoid the crush. Count on spending at least 25€ at any of these places unless you are careful. If the price of your fish is not on the menu, ask for it; fish is usually expensive and priced by the kilogram. Liotrivi (tel. 22980/72-269), in the Old Harbor, is a great place for simple grilled fish or *makaronada tou psara* (fish, tomato sauce, and pasta) or *mayiatiko a la Spetsiate* (fish stewed with tomatoes and herbs).

For standard Greek taverna food, including a number of vegetable dishes, try the rooftop taverna Lirakis, Dapia, over the Lirakis supermarket (tel. 22980/72-188), with a nice view of the harbor. To Kafeneio, a long-established coffeehouse and ouzo joint, on the harborfront, is a good place in which to sit and watch the passing scene, as is To Byzantino. Or try Orloff, on the road to the Old Harbor, which has a wide variety of *mezedes*. The island's popularity with tour groups seems to have led to a decline in the quality of restaurant fare.

Spetses has some of the best bakeries in the Saronic Gulf; all serve a Greek specialty beloved on the islands: *amygdalota,* small, usually crescent-shaped almond cakes, flavored with rosewater and covered with powdered sugar. It's usually served with a tall glass of cold water; you'll realize why when you bite into all that powdered sugar!

Patralis Taverna
Phone 22980-75380

Here's a place that gives the lie to that hoary old saying "you get what you pay for". In the surprisingly pricey town of Spetses, this traditional taverna has some of the best prices for seafood, and the freshest fish around. In fact, we'd say this is THE place to go in Spetses if you have a hankering for sea urchin, pasta with crab or lobster, or grilled red mullet. You may want to go for any sort of fish done "A la Spetsiota", a family recipe that's quite good. The verandah of the restaurant has wonderful sea views.

Trehantiri Bar Restaurant
For a romantic night out, try this bar and restaurant with top-notch food and service on the coastal road to Paleo Limani. The sign is hard to discern in English (it says tpexanthpi in Greek), but the bar and restaurant is around the corner and upstairs from a pizzeria bar. The late shipping magnate Stavros Niarchos whose island, Spetsopoula, is not far away was a frequent patron here.

## Best Nightlife in Spetses
Spetses has plenty of bars, discos, and bouzouki clubs from the Dapia to the Old Harbor to Ayia Marina, and even to the more remote beaches. For bars, try golden oldies Bratsera or Stavento, in the heart of Dapia. For discos, there's Figaro, with a seaside patio and international funk until midnight; afterward, the music switches to Greek, and the dancing follows suit, often until dawn.

The 1800 Bar & Internet Café, in Kounoupitsa, Spetses town, is the place to go if you want to listen to music, keep an eye on a TV, check your e-mail, and take in the narghile lounge, where you can smoke a water pipe, with some flavored tobacco, for 2 hours (10€). Fox often has live Gr

## Flora & Fauna

Flora

Greece may be a small country, but it is big on flora. It has the richest range of flora than any other European country, numbering more than 6,000 species. What is also surprising is that about 10 per cent are entirely unique. This means that they are *only* to be found in Greece and no-where else in the world!

Spetses contains a beautiful snapshot of many of these species and all year, evidence of this can be seen. Spring though, is when the island really comes alive. Every hillside, open space, courtyard and garden boasts a wide variety of plant life and colour is everywhere.

Two thirds of the island is covered in pine trees (mainly Aleppo Pine) belonging to the Anargyros Trust. In the hills, you can sometimes see small tins beneath the pines, collecting resin from cuts made in the trunk of the tree. This resin is used to make Retsina - the well known Greek wine. However, Retsina has lost popularity over recent years, with more upmarket Greek wines (made in vinyards from all over Greece) taking the market share.

On the sunny terraces in the hillsides, cereals, wild olives and almonds are cultivated and oranges, lemons, vines and loquats are grown in private courtyards and gardens. Spetses also has an abundance of fig trees, pistachios, oleander, myrtle, Carob and Chaste trees. A few imports from the past include Eucalyptus, Acacia and Melia, as well as Bougainvillea, Wisteria and Jacaranda.

There are far too many to list here, although it is important to note the wealth of aromatic herbs. These include thyme, marjoram, savory and rosemary (also Jerusalem Sage - although not used for cooking here).

As mentioned in the Geography section, it has been suggested that the island's abundance of aromatic herbs may have prompted the Venetians to name it Spetses, as *spezie* is the Italian word for spices.

## Spring Flora

April Waysides and May Day Wreaths
Well, of all the months to get your gardening clothes on and trowels in hand, this is the one- April the busiest gardening month in the Greek calendar. There is such a vast amount of work to do

what with tidying up after the winter and making sure that everything is just right for the long and incredibly dry summer. Not to mention any seeds that may still need to be sewn and weeds that may need to be weeded!

The flowers are also at their busiest in April, with a huge amount of blooming going on, therefore ensuring that waysides, hillsides and scrubland certainly are at their prettiest. March asphodels are withering, but all kinds of other bright and colourful flora are popping up all around, including the Corn Poppy! This is a beautiful sight fields of scarlet poppies, swaying in the spring breeze or as a mass of red behind an old whitewashed wall, which makes a warm and contrasting sight. Slightly less common, is the Long-Headed Poppy, which tends to come out a little later and is more pink than red. Take care though, one brush of the hand is enough to see their pretty petals fall to the ground!

Another spectacular sight is the simple but very delightful Rock Rose (also known as Cistus). Seen in abundance at this time of the year, across meadow land, pine forest, hill and mountain side the purple grey-leaved Cistus and the white Gum Sistus and Sage-leaved Sistus, are bushy evergreen shrubs that are looked upon as weeds in Greece. Hardy and long flowering, they survive well into early summer. Their orangey-yellow centres give a great look of depth to their rather papery petals and their thyme-scented perfume is truly Greek. The Gum Cistus is grown for its resin, ladanum, which is used as a base for various medications and some perfumes.

Out and about you may catch sight of locals collecting great bunches of chamomile flowers. This is for chamomile tea, which is not only popular for its taste, but also as a cure for all ails! From tummy aches, sore eyes and wounds it's a favourite Greek remedy...It is also used for a more aesthetically pleasing pastime that of the great May 1st 'stefani' (wreath). Being a national holiday, the custom is to get out into the countryside and collect spring flowers for the wreath and to hang it on the door until 24th June. (the feast day of St. John the Baptist). It is an extremely sociable event as friends will often go back to each other's houses to make them. School children will also make a wreath to take home to their parents, so front and back doors will always find themselves adorned! This national holiday really signifies the end of bad weather and the promise of better months ahead, and there is a general feeling of excitement and well being on this day.

Certainly well before May, but looking pretty good during this month, is the large bushy, shrubby perennial, Marguerite (Chrysanthemum frutescuns) or Paris Daisy, as it's known. This dominates the countryside, along with its relative the Crown Daisy (Chrysantheemum coronaium) which is also one of the main flowers used for May day wreaths. The Greeks fondly name all these daisy-type flowers as Margaríta.

Even though by the middle of May most of the flowers are dying away, there is the welcome appearance of various summer vegetables, including all the ingredients of the tasty Greek dish called 'briam' (baked summer vegetables). These include courgettes, aubergines, peppers and tomatoes a sure sign that summer is on the way.

## Summer Flora

There's a definite feeling that summer has started in Greece, when swallows, swifts and house martins swirl from all around, flitting in and out of the nests that they are preparing for their young. Cicadas and grasshoppers start to 'chirrup' from all corners of the garden and from along the bushy waysides. Dragonflies skitter from pond to pool and the water is at last beginning to be warm enough for us all to wallow in...

This may conjure up a relaxing image, but for those with gardens full of flora, then this dry season can be the most difficult. A war...and not only of the roses! Which plants will survive and which will die. The tasks of continuous watering, deadheading and weekly feeding for annuals, become an absolute must.

Showers are usually over by the first week of June. There may be unexpected thunderstorms, but that's just what they are not expected... Automatic watering systems can be a great investment for larger flowerbeds (although it is worth keeping an eye on these, as they can be temperamental, due to electrical cuts and pipe damage etc). To avoid the water running down and away on bigger plots with slopes, it is a good idea to terrace them. It is advisable to water well on a weekly basis, rather than little and often, so that the water can reach the bottom of the soil and encourage a deeper root system. Pots need to be watered on a daily basis and early morning is best so that the plants are still moist when photosynthesis occurs.

In these warm months, a lot of tender loving care is absolutely essential and daily deadheading, although sometimes tedious, is necessary. This ensures that flowers keep their shape and continue to bloom for as long as possible, keeping your gardens bright and cheery.

With spring, and its marvellous show of bright and vibrant colour, just over it is easy to assume that this dry Greek summer may be ready to sport a rather dead and withered appearance. This is, however, not necessarily so. Parts of southern Greece (particularly the more sheltered islands) are lucky to have gardens, courtyards and balconies with an array of rainbow coloured plants and shrubs, that bloom well into the month of July.

When seeding and planting in late winter/early spring, it is a good idea to include some of the following:

Lilies: Madonna and the Regal in particular, are incredibly beautiful and double up with their heady fragrance on warm summer evenings. The Regal is easy to grow, manages well in pots and is happy in the shade.

Plumbago auriculata: a shrub which spreads or climbs. The flowers are usually pale blue (although also white) and can be successfully seeded before going on to enjoy a life of full sunlight. Their bracts are slightly sticky and may happily stick to clothing.

Larkspur: a wild flower but very popular in gardens or on balcony pots. It is deep blue and stands tall and erect.

Lantana hybrids: evergreens with extremely bright colours of which pink with yellow and orange with yellow are most often seen. They need little water and bloom all summer through to autumn. Beware though, they do not smell very pleasant and their berries are poisonous.

Petunias (F1 hybrids): in almost every colour even stripey and starred. Easy to grow and enjoy full sun, but need feeding regularly. Potted together, with a few pansies, they make a stunning sight along a white wall.

Not forgetting, some good old Greek favourites , such as fruit trees lemons, oranges and kumquats; the summer flowering hibiscus; the exotic, climbing bougainvillea with a choice of vivid colours; the popular and hardy geranium;the pink, white and dark red oleander (with its one disadvantage of being very poisonous) and the beautifully scented, climbing roses and jasmine.

## Autumn Flora

On hillsides, in woodlands, along waysides in clumps and clusters under small bushes and between rocks the Cyclamen are now well established and can be seen everywhere in abundance. Their delicate and rich pink flowers stretch upwards on long, thin stems, as if trying to reach for the watery blue skies of October. Their dark green, marbled and veined leaves start to uncurl slightly later, followed by the flower stalks coiled into tiny little spirals, trying hard to protect the fruit inside.

Of the twenty species of Cyclamen, the Greek Sowbread, along with the Ivy-leaved Sowbread are both autumn flowering, as opposed to other types that flower in late winter and early spring. Growing equally well in a dry garden as in the wild, normal seed sowing should take place in October-November, with seeds needing as much as ten hours to soak beforehand.

However, moving the actual plant from the wild to the garden is not often successful, as they do not like to be moved. When buying an established Cyclamen they can happily stay in pots all winter, although you will have to create similar conditions to that of their natural habitat. Occupying the corner of a balcony, terrace or on a windowsill with as much light as a winter Mediterranean woodland, should be enough to ensure good, continued growth. If however, it turns yellow in late spring, then this is nothing to worry about as it will not be too late to re-plant it in the garden. Just stop watering it and move the corm from its now dry soil and wait until it pops its head above ground again the following autumn. A good place would be under deciduous trees, the bottom of stone walls or in flower beds.

Not only very pink and very pretty, in ancient Greece, the Cyclamen was very popular as a remedy. Greek writers and physicians proclaimed its healing benefits and the tuber juice was used on wounds and boils and also during childbirth. It was thought to bring good luck and serve as an aphrodisiac too and in those times was known as chelonian. This was after the Greek word chelona, meaning tortoise, as it was thought that its tubers bore a likeness to that of the small creature. The modern name however could possibly be a derivation from the Greek word kyklos, meaning circle. This was probably named as such, due to the rounded tuber or rolled up stalk. From past to present and then on to the future, the Cyclamen if looked after well can survive anything up to fifty years and may well be around long enough to see you re-potted!

Of the 80 worldwide species of Crocus, the equally delightful, autumn blooming Crocus Boryi, with its flowers of white and purple and yellow tongue can also be seen all over hillsides and along paths and walkways, happily sprouting from hard soil. Plant in late summer for autumn flowering, and make sure they lie about 5cm under the ground. Many self-seed but to be sure, take cormlets off existing crocus and plant when dormant. Flowers will close at night and on days with cloud but on those bright sunny days throughout October and November they will thrive.

All in all, November is definitely the busiest month for gardening. A time for seedlings (from September sown seeds) to be planted...a time for easy digging in soft ground ensured by the October rains...a time when days are still warm enough to guarantee swift growth of small trees and shrubs just planted or moved...a time to enjoy the warm midday sun before the cold weather strikes and sets in for the winter.

## Winter Flora

*FESTIVE FLORA.reds and oranges for Christmas and the New Year*
What could be better than natural Christmas decorations? The red berries of the holly and the white of the mistletoe are synonymous with the festive season, but in Greece there are plenty of seasonal fruits and flowers with their striking reds and oranges to brighten up the balcony, veranda or the garden.

Festive traditions too smashing a pomegranate on the doorstep to leave the abundant seeds inside to scatter across the floor, as the seeds of good fortune. This may be considered just as much fun as kissing under the mistletoe! The Pomegranate or Punica a native from Asia was naturalised in Greece and other parts of the Mediterranean a very long time ago. The fruit grows on rounded, deciduous small trees that can grow between 3 and 5 metres high. Bright green leaves sprout in the spring through to autumn, often giving the tree a spiny, shrub-like appearance.

Tubular shaped flowers open in early summer too and remain until early autumn. The winter fruits are as large as oranges, about 7-10 cm in diameter. The skin is leathery in texture and is a deep orange-red, which can quickly turn to brown. The edible part of the fruit, has a red-white flesh, but with many seeds making it quite difficult to eat. The leaves turn golden and the colourful fruits, against this leafy backdrop, make a beautiful winter garden decoration. When picked and brought inside, they can be left until they dry out, and then sprayed gold or silver. Pomegranate also has some very important healing qualities, such as gargling the juice to combat sore throats. In ancient Greece it was prescribed as an aphrodisiac, a stomach sedative and a cure for intestinal parasites. These qualities gave it its name as a symbol of life for the ancient Greeks and female Gods such as Demeter, Hera, Aphrodite and Persephone also revered the fruit.

One of my personal December- January favourites has to be the small evergreen tree the Kumquat (also known as Kinkon). This slow-growing tree is also a native to Asia, but grows very well in warm climates such as the Mediterranean. Reaching a height of between 3 to 4.5 metres, the evergreen leaves are alternately arranged along the stem and each measure between 2-7 cm. On top, they are darker green and finely toothed and on the underside they are slightly lighter in colour, resembling other citrus trees, such as the lemon and orange. The small oval fruits, appearing from December and lasting until about June, are between 2-5 cm long and have a leathery orange (slightly yellow) skin. The outside is sweet tasting, although the inner flesh can be slightly bitter, sometimes invoking a screwed up face when trying them for the first time! They are excellent in fruit salad or to be eaten as a dessert, jelly, jam, marmalade, syrup or even candied sweet. Used as a sweet sauce for meat dishes, I discovered that they make a tasty and unusual accompaniment too. In some countries, branches are cut and taken inside for Christmas decorations. In summer they keep looking good, as their delicate white flowers also create a pretty effect.

Definitely not edible, but firmly festive, is the Poinsietta (Euphorbia pulcherrima) a member of the Spurge family. Originating from Mexico, but happy in the Mediterranean climate where, growing out of doors or inside in pots, it can receive enough full sunlight and warmth to really flourish. Its vivid scarlet and green leaves have become a popular Christmas symbol almost as well known as the holly.

## Fauna

Fauna describes the total number of animal species existing in one particular geographical area. These include vertibrates and invertibrates. Fauna in Greece has not been studied to the extent of other countries, but it is thought that there are approximately 50,000 species in total. About 25% of these are endemic to Greece.

An approximate breakdown of species would be as follows:

✓ Land and freshwater species - over 23,000

✓ Sea species - over 3,500

✓ Insects make up the rest of the species, including some that have been recorded, but not yet listed.

✓ The main reasons for this biodiversity are:

✓ That Greece gave shelter to many of these (now endemic) species from Northern Europe, during the ice ages.

✓ The mild climate that permits insect activity during all of the year.

✓ Remote areas on the edges of peninsulas, where up to 45% of endemic species are found.

✓ The geographical position and the wide range of habitats and ecosystems existing in Greece, such as: wetlands; fertile shallows; old growth forests; caves; gorges; mountains and thousands of islands.

It goes without saying that urbanisation of particular areas means that certain species are on the edge of extinction or, have already become extinct.

There is no statistical evidence of species in Spetses available, but once again, as with flora, Spetses provides a healthy snapshot.

# Religion and Ethnic Influences

## Greek Orthodox Church on Spetses Island Greece

Visitors are always welcome, regardless of their denomination, to attend services at the main churches of the island.

Even when there isn't a service and if the church is open, visitors are welcome to enjoy looking inside or to take the opportunity for some quiet meditation. The churches are not museums but working places of worship and visitors should respect customs and not wear immodest attire, speak loudly or take photos of the interiors. Ladies if you sit down, remember not to cross your legs as it is deemed immodest.

## Greek Orthodox Name Days & Dates

According to Greek Orthodox tradition, every day of the year is dedicated to a Christian saint or martyr. January 7 for example, is the day of Saint John the Baptist and it is the name day for all Greek people named Yannis (or Ioannis = John, male) or Yanna (or Ioanna, female).

A person's Name Day is considered more important than the same person's actual birthday and it is always celebrated in Greece.

## How do Greek people celebrate their name days?

Firstly, they will probably go the church or chapel bearing their name e.g If their name is Dimitris, they will go to the church service in the morning at Ayios Dimitrios, where the church will be beautifully decorated with flags, flowers and special icons and candles.

If a friend of yours has a name day, then you should give him them call and wish them "Chronia Polla". If this is translated, then it means "Many Years" and it is a wish for good health and prosperity. You should ask them if they will accept visits at their house.

For birthday parties people invite their friends to their house for a drink or a birthday party but for name days this does not apply. It is up to you to visit your friend and wish them well for their name day. Bringing a gift is necessary. Flowers or liquor are ok, as well as books, music CDs or something more personal. It is also possible that your friend will invite you to a taverna or a bar on his name day. or may even have a name day party at their house. A gift is welcome in this case too.


## Active Pursuits in Spetses
Beaches
Ayia Marina, signposted and about a 30-minute walk east of Spetses town, is the best, and busiest, town beach. It has a number of tavernas, cafes, bars, including the locally famous Paradise, and discos. West of Spetses town, Ayii Anaryiri has one of the best sandy beaches anywhere in the Saronic Gulf, a perfect C-shaped

cove lined with trees, and, increasingly, almost more bars and tavernas than trees. The best way to get here is by water taxi. Paradise beach is crowded, littered, and, for me at least, not very appealing. Now, I hate to mention this, as all of us travel writers try to keep some secrets, but Zageria is as undeveloped a beach as you will find here. If you are interested, ask around for directions. Whichever beach you pick, go early, as beaches here get seriously crowded by midday.

Fans of *The Magus* may want to have a look at the beach at Ayia Paraskevi, which is bordered by pine trees. Located here are a cantina and Villa Yasemia, residence of the Magus himself. West over some rocks is the island's official nudist beach.

## The Beaches Inside Spetses
Around the town of Spetses there are scattered beautiful, blue beaches, which permits to the locals and visitors to enjoy their swim, close to the main port.

Most of the beaches are organised, with sun umbrellas and sun decks and are located near taverns and cafe.

Starting from the SE area of the island, we will meet the sandy beach of Agia Marina, 2 klm. from the Dapia port. Agia Marina is a well organised and popular beach with tavernas and beach bar in an evergreen environment.

Continuing our route through "Dapia", we come across the beach of Agios Nikolaos a small beach with sand and thin pebble, with crystal waters and quiet environment.

Continuing on we meet the sandy organised beach of Agios Mamas, with sun umbrellas, sun chairs and lots of people. Also the beach is in front of bars, restaurants and cafes, servicing many customers.

After "Dapia", west from the port, we meet the beach of Kounoupitsa, a small, marvelous beach from pebbles and sand with blue waters, which is also ideal for walking amongst the small fishing boat and for eating in various tavernas and shopping, all these along the beach's length.

Emmediately after the "Anagreirios" beach , is located and its length is 800 meters.

It is one of the most organised beaches in Spetses, with sun chairs, sun umbrellas, sea sports and restaurants.

Part of this beach is called "Kaiki Beach", with sun umbrellas and chairs, beach service, towels, beach volley, two beach bars and a restaurant.

## The Beaches outside Spetses Town
Outside the town of Spetses, you will meet organised beaches in beautiful natural coves with blue-green waters.

There you can enjoy, along with your swim, the water sports and other activities.

From the NE side of the island and going towards the SW, leaving from the beaches inside Spetses, we meet first the beach Kouzounos, across the ever green Spetsopoula isl. This beach is one of the most quiet and natural beaches on Spetses, with clean waters, colourful pebbles and ideal for swimming.

To the beach you are going with regular public bus, its starting point at the St.Mamas sqr., from May till the end of September.

Next, we meet the Ksilokeriza beach, a seclusive, organized beach with sand and pebbles, to the south side of the island. It is an ideal choice fort hose who want to swim in a lush natural surrounding and relax on the beautiful sandy beach.

On the beach you go with the same bus, whose starting point, from the town of Spetses, is located in the square of St. Mamas, from May until the end of September. Also with boats that organize day trips.

Southwest of Spetses town, about 10 km from the center, is the beach Agion Anargiron, an organized, busy beach with sand and pebbles, with deep water, suitable for water sports.

The beach is located in a beautiful, green bay and has facilities for water sports and other activities, and there are several restaurants and cafes.

Near the beach of St. Anargiron lies the sea cave "Bekiris" in which Spetsiots militants hid their women and children to protect them from the Turks. Access to the cave is being done by a tree-lined path, which starts from the beach Agion Anargiron.

To the beach you are going with regular public bus, its starting point at the St.Mamas sqr., from May till the end of September. Also with boats that organize day trips .

Continuing our tour, we meet the piney Agia Paraskevi beach, 12 km from the center, an organized, crowded beach in a small bay on the west side of Spetses, with pine trees reach the sea. This is one of the most beautiful sandy-pebbly beaches, offering inside a rich natural environment with crystal clear waters, comforts and water sports facilities.
On the beach of Agia Paraskevi you can go with boats that organize day trips.

The last beach we meet, completing our ride on the NW side of Spetses is the Zogeria, a sandy beach with clear blue waters inside a pine tree area, in which there are some traditional taverns.

The beach Zogeria is one of the best beaches. The wonderful landscape with pine trees reaching the sea, crystal clear waters and tranquil environment, create a lovely image for your holiday.

In beach Zogeria you can go with boats that organize day trips

## Deserted Beaches
Around the island there are many small coves and beaches, which you can visit by a boat, or with motorbikes, with sea taxi or a car taxi, or also by walking there.

Ligoneri, Vrellos, the first beach of Zogeria, as we are coming from the Schools, Bithistamna, are the most famous deserted beaches on the island.

At the perimeter of the island there are small or large caves with its own history to the Liberation War against the Turks, which were utilised as a refuge and store.

Accessing the caves is being done only with boats and it is best to consult an expert or a human guide.

## Close Excursions
*A. Daily tours to the beaches by boat*

After Easter starts the schedules of the boats that leave from Dapia port, every day in the morning, and execute daily trips or go across to Kosta or to the west at the coast of Zogeria or towards the east to Saints Anargyrous and Agia Paraskevi beaches.

The boats are leaving at around 11.00 in the morning and come back around 17.00 in the afternoon.

*B. The circumnavigation of the island by boat or kaiki or water taxi*

You can rent a boat with outboard for 5 people in front of the Mansion of Economou in Kounoupitsa, or for larger groups, rent a boat or water taxi from the port of Dapia or from Kounoupitsa.

Leaving Ntapia we pass from Agios Mamas, the Mansions on the beach of Saint Nicholas, we pass the cape with the lighthouse on the Old Harbour and see the church of "Panagia Armata".

Then the blue church of Agios Dimitrios, the Gulf of Garifallo and further beyond the yellow church of Agia Marina with its beach. Up high you can see two monasteries facing each other and Spetsopoula to the south and the surrounding islands, with the church of St. John on the largest island of them.

After that, the Fanari of Lianokavou is located to the beach of Kouzounos and then as we see the beach Xylokeriza. Further beyond as we go towards Kasidokavo, we meet very beautiful and small bays and at the hilltop the church of Prophet Elia.

As we continue, appears the beach of Agion Anargiron, which has the largest sandy beach of the island, the cave "Bekiris" and then, after some time, the beach of Agia Paraskevi. As we continue at the northwest, passing by the cave of Zaira and Petrokaravo, we turn to the bay Kamares and we reach the bay of Zogeria.

Immediately after, there are the beaches of Zogeria, the cape of Palaiogiorgi and then the small bay of Vaizas. Further down, there is a steep coast and ahead lies the beach of Vrellos and then the beach Ligoneri.

Also we meet the Schools, the red chapel of Resurrection and then the Kounoupitsa beach, shortly before returning to Ntapia.

*C. Walk the paths of Spetses island*

Spetses is famous for its forest covering 40% of the island's surface. Unfortunately in recent years some was burned, but even now the visitor can admire the magnificent views of the island, to smell the pine, thyme, cranberries, heather, see wildflowers and look, if you know for herbs and mushrooms.

From Kastelli taking the road that goes to the church of St. Saviour and of St. Dimitri, we continue at the left the paved road, we pass from the water tanks and we are in St. Hadrian's church.

Further down is a large stone house the "Port Arthur", as it was called, and during the course of our route we will meet at the right, the beautiful church of Agia Markella and higher always at our right hand, the one of the Panagia Kapsodematousa which celebrates on July 2.

Going the same way we will meet the reserve-house of the hunters, while 300 meters west is the location "Vigla" with a tower for monitoring fire.

The Refuge-house of the hunters is located in the back of the mountain, from which we see both sides of the island. The view from there is wonderful.

Immediately after there is a crossing where there are two paths to the left and one which goes ahead.

The first road to the left leads to the "Xara", the home of the sisters Mary and Eirini Botassi with the small church of the "Three Spetsiots", at the left of which there is a small path that leads to the fountain "Sikia", from which we continue and reach the first houses of the village of Spetses, if we want to go from this point in the city.

Continuing the first route to the left, we go to the hill of Elona with the church of Holy Virgin of Elona at the top, from which we descend in the regional area "Kosmadaki", which is the tomb of the monk Akakios Koutsi.

206

The second road to the left, goes down to the beach of Agios Ananrgyron after 3 kilometers.

Following the road that goes in front, at the right side we find a fairly wide path that leads to the observation station ,originally made by the Italians in order to monitor Spetses isl. and today observatory for the volunteers protectors of the forest during the summer.

Continuing the path in front of the observatory we arrive at "Daskalakis" estate with the chapel of Holy Virgin, where is a celebration at the 1rst of September.

Continuing the road and leaving the path with the observatory we will arrive after one kilometer, to the Prophet Elijah the highest mountain point of Spetses.

We climb towards the chapel with thw same name to enjoy the view and drink some water from the cistern. Southwest we view the town and see the mountain "Parnona" while at the northwest we view "Tolo" , towards the north the "Kranidi" and the mountain "Didimo".

There are trails and roads leading to all the famous beaches of the island and during the walk, visitors will stop many times to admire the unique view to the sea, the coast of the Peloponnese, the islands and the endless pine trees with wonderful scents of the forest.

## D. Another route to the Monasteries of Spetses

From Dapia, and at the left , we find the square Roloi and following the internal road we reach the church of Agios Eleftherios.

Here the road splits in two directions and the southeastern route leads in "Kokkinaria" and continuing leads to the monastery of Agion Panton.

Before the monastery of Agion Panton there is an intersection, that to the left leads to the monastery of Panagia "Gorgoepikoos".

The same road continues beyond the Monaseri to the east, and from a point and then becomes a path that goes parallel to the main road, having at his opposite the small island Spetsopoula, leading to the Elona, from there to "Xara" and to the house of the hunters.

From here we go to the "Daskalakis" estate with the chapel of Holy Virgin, and then after 1 km, to the the Prophet Elijah.

## E. Daily trips to locations around Spetses

By flying dolphin in the morning you can go to Porto Heli, or Hermione, or even in Hydra and Poros and return to Spetses again in the afternoon with the flying dolphin.

## Planning a Trip in Spetses

### Getting There

Daily hydrofoil and ferry service to Spetses and other Saronic Gulf islands is offered by Hellenic Seaways (tel. 210/419-9200). Saronikos Ferries (tel. 210/417-1190) takes passengers and cars to Aegina, Poros, and Spetses; cars are not allowed to disembark on Hydra. Euroseas (tel. 210/411-3108) has speedy catamaran service from Piraeus to Poros, Hydra, and Spetses. For information on schedules, you can try one of the various numbers of the Piraeus Port Authority (tel. 210/412-4585, 210/422-6000, or 210/410-1480), but phones are not always answered. On Spetses, try tel. 22980/72-245 is a useful site for ferry schedules as is(gtp.gr).

Visitor Information

The island's travel agencies include Alasia Travel (tel. 22980/74-098) and Spetses & Takis Travel (tel. 22980/72-215). Andrew Thomas's *Spetses* (Lycabettus Press), usually on sale on the island, is the book to get if you want to pursue Spetses's history.

Fast Facts in Spetses

The National Bank of Greece is one of several banks on the harbor with an ATM. Most travel agencies (9am-8pm) will also exchange money, usually at less favorable rates than banks. The local health clinic (tel. 22980/72-201) is inland from the east side of the port. The police (tel. 22980/73-100) and tourist police (tel. 22980/73-744) are to the left off the Dapia pier, where the hydrofoils dock, on Boattassi. The port authority (tel. 22980/72-245) is on the harborfront. The post office is on Boattassi near the police station; it's open from 8am to 2pm Monday to Friday. The telephone office (OTE), open Monday to Friday from 7:30am to 3pm, is to the right off the Dapia pier, behind Hotel Soleil. Internet access is available at Delphina Net-Café on the harborfront for 5€ an hour.

## Getting Around in Spetses

The island's limited public transportation consists of several municipal buses and a handful of taxis. Motorcycle and moped agents are required to, but do not always, ask for proof that you are licensed to drive such vehicles and give you a helmet. Be sure to check the tires and brakes; mopeds start at 15€ a day, motorcycles start at 20€ except on summer weekends, when the sky is the limit. Bikes are also widely available, and the terrain along the road around the island makes them a good means of transportation; three-speed bikes cost about 12€ per day, while newer 21-speed models go for about 15€. Horse-drawn carriages can take you from the busy port into the quieter back streets, where most of the island's handsome old mansions are located. Take your time choosing a driver; some are friendly and informative, others are surly. Fares are highly negotiable.

The best way to get to the various beaches around the island is by water taxi. Locals call it a *venzina* (gasoline); each little boat holds about 8 to 10 people. Here, too, fares are negotiable. A tour around the island costs about 50€. Schedules are posted on the pier. You can also hire a water taxi to take you anywhere on the island, to another island, or to the mainland. Again, prices are highly negotiable. Ayia Marina, about a 30-minute walk southeast of Spetses Town, is the best beach close to town and terribly popular; it's the place to see and be seen for a chic Athenian crowd, some of whom arrive in high style via horse and buggy. On the forested west coast, 6km (4 miles) west of Spetses Town, Ayii Anaryiri has one of the best sandy beaches anywhere in the Saronic Gulf, a perfect C-shaped cove lined with trees, but almost more bars and tavernas than greenery. Also on the west coast, about 10km (6 miles) west of Spetses Town, is the beach at Ayia Paraskevi, bordered by pine trees. The idyllic stretch of sand figures in The Magus, though it's no longer the isolated strand it once was. West over some rocks is the island's official nudist beach.

The End

Printed in Great Britain
by Amazon